Towards an Analysis of Discourse

of Discourse

The English used by teachers and pupils

J. McH. Sinclair and R. M. Coulthard

*Based on a report submitted to the Social Science
Research Council and written by J. McH. Sinclair,
I. J. Forsyth, R. M. Coulthard and M. C. Ashby.*

WITHDRAWN FROM
THE LIBRARY

UNIVERSITY OF
WINCHESTER

LONDON
OXFORD UNIVERSITY PRESS
1975

KA 0041814 5

Oxford University Press, Ely House, London W1

GLASGOW NEW YORK TORONTO MELBOURNE WELLINGTON
CAPE TOWN IBADAN NAIROBI DAR ES SALAAM LUSAKA ADDIS ABABA
DELHI BOMBAY CALCUTTA MADRAS KARACHI LAHORE DACCA
KUALA LUMPUR SINGAPORE HONG KONG TOKYO

ISBN 019 436011 3

© *Oxford University Press 1975*

*This book is sold subject to the condition that it shall not, by way of
trade or otherwise, be lent, re-sold, hired out, or otherwise circulated
without the publisher's prior consent in any form of binding or cover
other than that in which it is published and without a similar
condition including this condition being imposed on the subsequent
purchaser.*

KING ALFRED'S COLLEGE
WINCHESTER

37.102
SIN | 52680

*Printed in Great Britain by
W. & J. Mackay Ltd., Chatham, Kent.*

CONTENTS

ACKNOWLEDGEMENTS

This work is based on research carried out at the University of Birmingham between 1970 and 1972 and supported by a grant from the Social Science Research Council. As indicated on the title page, a report was produced at the time, but continuation of the work and the interest aroused by the circulation of the report in mimeo prompted us to prepare an updated and much revised version for publication. Our major debts are to our research team, who not only carried out much of the work but prepared substantial parts of the original report. Ian Forsyth was the senior member of the team and Margaret Ashby joined us in the second year. We would like to acknowledge also the help of two groups of people without whom the work would have been difficult if not impossible. One is the teachers who allowed us to record their lessons, and Miss D. Atkinson of Coventry College of Education who introduced us to several of them—as it is our practice to keep them anonymous, we cannot acknowledge our debt to them by name. The other group is our Advisory Committee, chaired by George Perren, C.I.L.T., and consisting of Mr. T. M. Brown, Moray House College of Education; Mrs. A. Pope, S.S.R.C.; Professor J. Regan, Claremont Graduate School; Professor W. P. Robinson, Macquarie University; Professor P. H. Taylor, Birmingham University; Dr. E. Tonkin, Birmingham University; and Dr. H. G. Widdowson, Edinburgh University.

1 INTRODUCTION

This monograph describes the findings of a research project, *The English Used by Teachers and Pupils*, sponsored by the Social Science Research Council between September 1970 and August 1972, which set out to examine the linguistic aspects of teacher/pupil interaction. We were interested in such questions as: what function does a given utterance have—is it a statement, question, command, or response—and how do the participants know; what type of utterance can appropriately follow what; how and by whom are topics introduced and how are they developed; how are 'turns' to speak distributed and do speakers have differing rights to speak?

The research project was one stage in a continuing investigation of language function and the organization of linguistic units above the rank of the clause. Both of these have been traditional concerns of British linguistics, stressed by Malinowski (1935) and Firth (1935), but were neglected during the 1960's partly because of the immense problems involved and partly because the intellectual climate was unfavourable.

American structuralists and transformationalists alike had concentrated massively and very successfully on problems within phonology and the grammar of the clause, and put aside attempts to deal with paragraphing or meaning. Verbal and non-verbal context were ignored as having little bearing on grammatical or phonological description. Transformational linguistics developed as a science by inferring from the data of actual usage a well-defined object—a uniform and homogeneous language structure, discovered in the competence of all native speakers and therefore capable of study in the productions of any one individual, usually the linguist himself.

Although there were some linguists who saw language as a series of interrelated levels mediating, and showing the relationships, between context and phonetic substance (Halliday *et al.* 1964, Lamb 1966), the concerns of most linguists were much narrower and were reflected in the model proposed by Chomsky (1965). It aims to show how a given phonetic realization has a grammatical structure and a meaning—but there is a major difference in the concept of meaning. Firth suggests that

the principal components of . . . meaning are phonetic func-

1

tion, which I call a 'minor' function, the major functions—lexical, morphological, and syntactical . . . , and the function of a complete locution in the context of situation, or typical context of situation, the province of semantics. (1935)

Chomsky's mid-sixties model completely ignores Firth's semantics and in so doing is able to ignore both performance and higher units of structure. Problems such as the lack of fit between a grammatical structure, e.g. *interrogative*, and a contextual type, e.g. *question*, can all be avoided. How, for example, does a hearer know when a declarative structure has the function of a question, and how does he know that a clause asks or does not ask a question depending on where it occurs in a sequence of clauses? If one ignores problems of this kind one's model is free to concentrate on generating a series of grammatical structures into which lexical items can later be slotted. The function of the semantic component is simply to produce an interpretation after relating grammatical and lexical information.

Most transformational work concentrated on the grammatical component and the inadequacies of this approach to meaning only gradually emerged. Katz and Fodor (1963) demonstrated incidentally the insurmountable problems of trying to define lexical meaning independent of context, and could only suggest the most trivial of functions for the semantic component, while Weinreich's much more complex system found little favour. Eventually the tail came to wag the dog. Increasing problems with the semantic description of sentence have led Ross, the Lakoffs and McCawley to a realization of the necessity to consider the presuppositions behind clauses and some of the contextual constraints on meaning.

The approach proposed by Sinclair (1966) was diametrically opposite to Chomsky's. He suggested examining real examples with all their performance features. He focused on questions and answers and suggested that only by examining the context in which an utterance is produced, the presuppositions behind the utterance, the intention of the speaker and respondent, and the evidence available to a decoder, can one really understand the meaning of an utterance.

This early work also stressed paragraphing in spoken discourse. Conversations are everyday examples of the fact that several participants can jointly produce coherent texts; utterances and parts of utterances relate back and forwards, place certain restrictions on what can occur and affect how preceding or succeeding items are interpreted. Sinclair (1968) went on to examine the relationship between the grammatical structure of an utterance and its function in discourse. Questions, for instance, can have a declarative, interrogative, imperative, or moodless structure. There are often features in the situation, such as relative status of participants, which will determine which form is most appropriate on that occasion and also how a less appropriate form will be interpreted—as cheekiness, condescension, sarcasm, and so on.

This functional approach to language was adapted experimentally in research carried out during 1968. The aim of the research was to discover the ways in which West Indian children and working-class English children differed in their linguistic behaviour and abilities from middle-class English children. The fashionable method for measuring disadvantage was to collect samples of speech and sometimes writing from both groups of children and to discover differences in the frequency with which they exploited the options provided by the linguistic system. The major drawbacks of using such performance data are firstly and obviously that a child who does not use a particular structure need not necessarily be unable to use it, but may simply not have felt the need to use it in the context. Secondly and more seriously, despite the efforts of the 'sentence stretchers' (Boesen 1966), there is no principled reason why grammatical complexity should be 'better'.

To approach the assessment and measurement of disadvantage from a different angle Wight and Norris (1970) and Coulthard (1970) devised a series of Language Function Tests. Children were asked to use language to get another child to perform a task such as selecting the correct card from a set, or building a tower of bricks. These Language Function Tests involved the children in describing, directing and explaining and the children were compared not on grammatical complexity, or breadth or even appropriacy of vocabulary, but on how successful they were—could they use the resources of their language to achieve an end, and how long did it take them. Both tests and measurement were crude but show the beginning of the current emphasis on communicative, and not simply linguistic, competence (Hymes 1972, Candlin 1972, Widdowson 1971).

At the same time work was proceeding on the analysis of conversation. Firth (1935) had observed that in conversation 'we shall find the key to a better understanding of what language really is, and how it works'. Our interests again were in the

3

function of utterances and the structure of discourse. We were looking for answers to such questions as: how are successive utterances related; who controls the discourse; how does he do it; how, if at all, do other participants take control; how do the roles of speaker and listener pass from one participant to another; how are new topics introduced and old ones ended; what linguistic evidence is there for discourse units larger than the utterance? In looking for answers to these questions, however, we began to suspect that desultory conversation was perhaps the most sophisticated and least overtly rule-governed form of spoken discourse and therefore almost certainly not the best place to begin. In normal conversation, for example, changes of topic are unpredictable. Participants are of equal status and have equal rights to determine the topic. Thus, while one speaker can usually control the direction of the discourse as long as he is actually talking, a succeeding speaker who is bored, bemused, or has something only partly relevant that he wants to contribute, can change the topic completely.

In the following example, utterance 1 is the ending of the topic 'rifles'. All the speakers apparently agree that everything they want to say about rifles has been said and they try to establish another topic. But of course each speaker has the right of veto. First 'driving' and then 'discipline' are rejected until they agree on 'drilling', introduced in utterance 8, which continues for the next dozen utterances.

1. S1   We got these exercises and you're to take the butt and hold point it away up there and we couldn't. Our arm used to shoot up and down it came.

2. S2   Well I joined for these reasons and plus the driving you get taught you're taught to drive.

3. S3   Well also my father said I need a bit of discipline you know.

4. S1   There's none there.

5. S2   You won't get any there honestly it's just terrific.

6. S3   That's why I'm joining it make him think I'm getting discipline.

7. S1   Oh it's great fun isn't it.

8. S2   Oh but wait have you been on a drilling yet?

9. S3   No.

10. S2   Just you wait.

(Text I)[1]

[1]The numbering of texts refers to the original research corpus and is maintained here and elsewhere in this book for convenience of reference.

There are of course techniques one can use in conversation to make it more likely that the discourse will continue on the lines you intend. For instance, speaker 2 would have increased the probability of speaker 3 accepting driving as the topic of utterance 3 by asking him a question, 'Can you drive?'. While anything *can* follow a question if the addressee is rude enough, speaker 2 would almost certainly have received a reply concerned with driving, though if speaker 3 had been determined to talk about discipline there is little more speaker 2 could have done; after answering the question the speaker need not surrender the initiative, but has the option of changing the topic:

'Yes I can but you see also my father said I need a bit of discipline you know.'

We felt the need to begin with a form of discourse which had more structure and direction.

A second difficulty with the analysis of desultory conversation, and also some more formal speech situations, is that a speaker can always sidestep and quarrel with a question instead of answering it, thus introducing a digression or a complete change of direction.

R.D.   Tell me Prime Minister don't you feel that you are now going to provoke the unions by making striking illegal?

P.M.   Look I must take issue with you again Robin that is precisely what we have not done if you read the White Paper properly.
(Midweek 18.1.73)

Such participant equality introduces added complications with which we did not feel ready to deal.

Thirdly, the ambiguity inherent in language means that people occasionally misunderstand each other; more often, and for a wide variety of reasons, people exploit the ambiguity and pretend to have misunderstood:

Father   Is that your coat on the floor again?

Son   Yes. (Goes on reading)

The father is using the resources of the language to avoid giving a direct command to his son; he uses a formulation which betrays irritation but is as far as he can go towards the polite 'Could you pick up your coat, please?' However, because he uses an interrogative formulation, his son is able to ignore the intended command and reply as if it were a question. Such play with and upon language occurs frequently in conversation and presents added difficulties.

With these and many other problems inherent in conversation we decided it would be more productive to begin again with a more simple type of spoken discourse, one which has much more overt structure, where one participant has acknowledged responsibility for the direction of the discourse, for deciding who shall speak when, and for introducing and ending topics. We also wanted a situation where all participants were genuinely trying to communicate, and where potentially ambiguous utterances were likely to have one accepted meaning. We found the kind of situation we wanted in the classroom. As Hymes later said,

> Studying language in the classroom is not really 'applied' linguistics; *it is really basic research*. Progress in understanding language in the classroom is progress in linguistic theory. (1972b)

In our effort to make things as simple as possible initially, we chose classroom situations in which the teacher was at the front of the class 'teaching', and therefore likely to be exerting the maximum amount of control over the structure of the discourse. While it was basic to our theory that the verbal and non-verbal context would affect the discourse, we had no theoretical basis for distinguishing between important and unimportant features and therefore set out to control as many of the potential variables as possible—age, ability, class size, teacher/pupil familiarity, topic of lesson.

Our initial sample consisted of the tapes of six lessons, all based on the hieroglyph materials reproduced in Appendix I, all taught to groups of up to eight 10–11-year-old children by their own class teacher. The system of analysis outlined in Chapter 3 was devised for and based on these lessons. However, once we felt able to handle the controlled sample, we collected a wide variety of tapes covering children of different age groups, in different schools, being taught different subjects by teachers with differing degrees of formality. The system required some, but not major, revision and is now able to cope with most teacher/ pupil interaction inside the classroom. What it cannot handle, and of course was not designed to handle, is pupil/pupil inter- action in project work, discussion groups, or the playground.

Armed with the results of this research, we are currently

attempting to specify a descriptive apparatus capable of greater generality. We have selected a small number of situations which contrast with the classroom along various dimensions but which all have clearly recognizable roles, objectives, and conventions. Chapter 5 gives a brief account of work in progress and indicates the main lines of a developing theory of language interaction. Publication of this volume is designed to promote the generalization of the descriptive apparatus by making it readily available to critics and fellow practitioners.

2 SHORT REVIEW OF THE LITERATURE

The research project set out to describe both the structure of one form of spoken discourse—that is the way in which units above the rank of clauses are related and patterned—and the way in which such language functions as statement, question, and command are realized through grammatical structure and position in the discourse. This chapter puts the present work into perspective against other work in the field. Certain important contributions are further described in Appendix II.

DISCOURSE STRUCTURE

In our search for a starting point we found very little within linguistics, which was mainly concerned with the description of language structure up to the rank of the clause. The clauses described almost never had a real context or cotext and when they did this was only seen as relevant in so far as it provided information useful for the description of the clause. Halliday's (1967) discussion of the information structure of the clause, and Hasan's (1968) discussion of such cohesion features as anaphora and exophora do depend on the concept of a contextualized clause, but are not concerned with the structure of the text. Items outside the clause are used to explain features inside the clause, but the existence of certain items within the clause which refer out to other clauses is not used to discuss the way in which larger units are structured.

Literary stylistics, although centrally concerned with the analysis of stretches of text, was similarly unproductive. Written texts of course differ quite radically from spoken; the amount of time available for composition permits extensive revision and consequently the production of a much more polished and highly organized text. This is reflected in the aims of the analysis. There are two major approaches within stylistics. One, concerned particularly with narrative, begins with the concept of a complexly organized text and attempts to show structure in terms of narrative, not linguistic, units. The analysis is based on the breakdown of the topic or content into episodes and events on which operations analogous to combination, transformation, embedding, and so on, can be performed (Chatman 1969, Todorov

1966, Barthes 1966). The other approach, beginning with the idea that the text has been carefully composed, looks at the grammatical choices the author has made, and discusses their literary effects and effectiveness (Halliday 1971, Sinclair 1966, 1968). Such analyses usually restrict themselves to the clause and below, although Short (1970), in examining conversation in literature, noted lexical cohesion in successive utterances by different speakers. He suggests that

> the dominated person will tend to use the items that the person in control gives him. Only if he tries to reverse the roles will he try to introduce new vocabulary. (p. 251)

In the research reported here we were unable to follow up this observation but we are now looking at lexical repetition as one indicator of the deep structure of discourse. This point is taken up in more detail in Chapter 5.

Non-literary stylistics has also concentrated on the clause in its attempt to distinguish styles of speech and writing. Joos (1962) proposes five styles ranging from formal to casual, while Halliday *et al.* (1964) suggest a large number of registers named after the *field* in which they occur, for example the 'register of advertising'. Registers are characterized by grammatical and more particularly lexical features—'cleanse' is characteristic of the language of advertising, 'probe into' that of newspapers, and so on. The only major attempt to define a register was by Huddleston *et al.* (1968) and concentrated on the grammatical features of sentences and clauses in scientific English.

There is of course no reason why the study of register should not have been tackled at the supra-sentential level, and our current work suggests that there are distinctive discourse structures for each of the situations we have so far investigated.

We see our work as primarily sociolinguistic although it differs markedly from most other work in sociolinguistics. Fishman (1968) formulates the major questions for the sociology of language as 'who speaks what to whom, when and to what end', and the majority of the research has been correlational, relating variations in certain features of the social structure to variations in features of language: phonetic (Labov 1964, 1966); grammatical and lexical (Bernstein 1962a, 1962b, Geertz 1960, Lawton 1968); the choice of one language code rather than another (Bernstein 1972, Gumperz 1964); the choice of one language rather than another (Rubin 1963).

The only attempt within sociolinguistics to describe the

structure of a spoken text is by Mitchell (1957) who describes the language of buying and selling in Cyrenaica. He divides transactions into a series of stages, and then discusses the features of the language typical of each of the stages. However, the stages are not isolated on linguistic criteria, there are no boundary markers and as 'stage is an abstract category, the numbering of stages does not necessarily imply a sequence in time'. In fact, stages are simply defined by the kind of activity that is appropriate to them. Neither does he attempt to provide a linguistic structure for the stages but simply characterizes them by the kinds of phrase and clause, often ritual, which occur within them. This was the very thing we wanted to avoid in our analysis of classroom discourse. It would have been easy to accept a pedagogical structure and then look at a unit like 'collecting dinner money' for typical phrases and expressions, but our interest was always in the linguistic structure of discourse.

Only the theoretical papers of Hymes (1962, 1964b, 1967, 1972) bore directly on what we were attempting. Since 1964 he has attempted to outline a programme for the integrated study of language and use, the ethnography of speaking. His aims are comprehensive, the description of communicative competence —how does a member of a community know when to speak and when to remain silent, which code to use when, where and how.

> Among the notions with which such a theory must deal are those of speech community, speech situation, speech event, speech act, fluent speaker, components of speech events, functions of speech, etc. (Hymes 1972a, p. 53)

This system is not exemplified by application to 'real' data but we can see in it the beginnings of an attempt to handle the structure of discourse in terms of larger and smaller units: 'an event may consist of a single speech act, but will often comprise several'. In our terms it constitutes a beginning, but consisting as it does of only two units ('events' do not combine to form 'situations', but simply occur in situations), it offers no real definition of the smallest unit.

> The speech act is the minimal term of the set just discussed ... It represents a level distinct from the sentence and not identifiable with any single portion of other levels of grammar, nor with segments of any particular size defined in terms of other levels of grammar. (*Ibid.* pp. 56–7)

10

Independently, as outlined in Chapter 3, we reached a similar position. For us also, discourse is a separate level, but we insist on a relatively small number of speech acts defined according to their function in the discourse and combining in predictable structures to form higher units.

LANGUAGE FUNCTIONS

Traditionally three major language functions, or contextual types, have been identified as statement, question and command, having their typical realizations in declarative, interrogative, and imperative forms. However, the relationship between these functions and forms in actual language use is more flexible—we can, for instance, use a declarative form to give a command or make a request.

Linguists have reacted differently to language functions. Bloomfield (1933), turned his back on the problem by observing that

> the statement of meanings is the weak point in language study, and will remain so until human knowledge advances far beyond its present state. (p. 140)

Transformational grammar by its very nature is unsuited to handling such context-dependent meanings, although Katz and Postal (1964) do discuss the case of the sentence 'You will go' which can be interpreted as a command, equivalent to 'I order you to go' or as a declarative statement. The deep grammar of this sentence ought to provide two analyses which will account for its surface ambiguity, and this problem has recently led to an explicit attempt to build the 'illocutionary force' or function of sentences into deep grammar. Boyd and Thorne (1969) discuss the illocutionary force of sentences containing modal verbs ('will', 'can', 'would', 'could', etc.) and give analyses of declarative surface structures, which suggest that their semantic deep structure is not always that of a statement. They argue, for example, that the modal verb 'will' is an indicator that the illocutionary potential of the sentence is a prediction.

Modal verbs play a large part in producing the lack of direct correlation between the three grammatical forms and functions mentioned, and it would certainly seem useful to pursue the possibility of reducing this lack of correlation by deep structure analyses. This would extend the range of that part of the meaning of an utterance which is derived from internal grammatical structure and is thus a constant base for all occasions of use. However, there is no need for the full meaning of sentences to be derivable from their internal structure together with lexical meaning, since the production of isolated sentences without a context is a pastime only of the linguist and not a characteristic use of language. Further, the flexibility and range of human meanings would be greatly restricted if this were the case. A large part of the meaning of a sentence must always be determined by the context in which it is uttered, even when the most elaborated grammatical structures and most specific lexical items are employed. Much of everyday language use is not designed to be verbally explicit, direct and literal, but can achieve its ends in subtle ways by reliance on features of context and a listener's procedures of interpretation using shared social conventions. We might account for the equivalence of 'Will you pick your coat up' and 'Pick your coat up' within a deep structure grammar, but to expect also to account for their equivalence in function with 'Is that your coat on the floor?' in the same way would be an attempt to ignore the social nature of meaning, and to put too much of social life into grammar. The model outline in Chapter 3 leaves open the possibilities raised by Boyd and Thorne and attempts to show how one particular context provides guides to the interpretation of grammatical structure.

Halliday's (1970) discussion of language structure and function is pitched at a different level. He is concerned not with the function or meaning of a given utterance of a sentence, but rather with the function of the presence and surface ordering of elements within a sentence. His approach draws on the work of the Prague linguists, particularly Vachek (1966) and Firbas (1959, 1964), towards a synthesis of structural and functional approaches in linguistics. Halliday insists that without an examination of grammar there is no reason for making any particular classification of language uses, unless one uses 'external' psychological or sociological generalizations about the uses of language. He finds in the structure of the clause three functions: (1) the 'ideational'—expressing content; (2) the 'interpersonal'—maintaining social relations; and (3) the 'textual' enabling links to be made with the situation and cohesive texts to be constructed. This approach to function did not provide us with a useful starting point. However, just as in Chapter 3 we return to *Categories of the Theory of Grammar* for a system of presenting our description so at some future time we may find this framework similarly useful. Halliday's textual component, which deals with the contextual relevance of elements of the clause, attempts to explain why the surface structure of a particular clause is as it is. One option is thematization, as previously pointed out by Firbas (1959, 1964). In English this is effected by placing the crucial elements of a message in first place in the sentence. This concept could deal, for example, with the difference between the following sentences:

1. They showed you a Pharaoh's body mummified on Blue Peter.
2. On Blue Peter they showed you a Pharaoh's body mummified.

In our system of analysis both these sentences, occurring at the same place in discourse structure, would be coded identically, as pupil-initiated *informing* moves. It is, however, not chance that it is the first not the second utterance which occurs in the text. The teacher's theme is Egyptian mummies, not TV programmes, and a pupil initiation is only likely to be successful if it is seen to be thematically relevant. Attention to such options as thematization could provide a more delicate description of the lowest functional units we identify. However, the level of language function in which we are centrally interested is neither the universal functions of language, nor the detailed function of surface formal ordering within the sentence. It is rather the level of the function of a particular utterance, in a particular social situation and at a particular place in a sequence, as a specific contribution to a developing discourse.

Linguists' conceptions of language functions, discussed above, represent an attempt to show how formal linguistic devices of a particular language are used to express distinctions of meaning and function. Questions of language function have also been discussed by philosophers. The concept of the 'illocutionary force' of an utterance used by Boyd and Thorne is drawn from the work on speech acts by Austin (1962) and Searle (1969).

Philosophy, like linguistics, has concentrated its attention on referential uses of language. Austin's work stems from an argument that various philosophical problems have been misformulated on the assumption that certain utterances are statements, when in fact they are performing an action, for example, promising. Much of Austin's work was devoted to attempting to find criteria for distinguishing those utterances which perform illocutionary acts from those which do not—a problem later abandoned with the realization that all utterances perform illocutionary acts as well as any referential act they may make. Arguments between Austin and Searle cannot concern us here and references will be mainly to the more recent discussion of speech acts by Searle.

A crucial distinction is between the 'sentence' and the 'act' it is used to perform. The unit of linguistic communication is not the symbol, word or sentence, but the production of those in the performance of an act. Searle sees a theory of language as part of a theory of action, requiring for completeness the study of the role of formal features in speech acts, to complement the independent study of form. The performance of speech acts, it is hypothesized, is made possible by certain rules for the use of linguistic elements. In equating rules for performing speech acts with rules for uttering linguistic elements, i.e. with the rules of meaning of sentences, Searle denies the usual divorce between or exclusive concentration on either sentence meaning or the situated use of expressions. It is insisted, against behaviourist theories of language use, that a speech act is performed in virtue of the conventional meaning of the sentence used. Philosophy however is not concerned with the conventional devices for promising, requesting, and so on, in a particular language. Searle suggests that those devices include performative verbs, for example 'I promise', intonation, stress and word order, but he is concerned with underlying rules which provide, for example, for the utterance of any promising device to count as the undertaking of an obligation. The resulting analysis of speech acts is thus in terms of the circumstances, intentions and expectations which must hold, universally, for a sentence including conventional promising devices to act as a promise.

Searle expects that specifications of those presuppositions for the innumerable varieties of speech acts we can refer to with performative verbs, such as threaten, greet, request, and so on, will be able to be organized into sets of core specifications which will provide a basis for grouping speech acts, but much work needs to be done before this can be seen as even a possibility.

Our concept of function differs from all those outlined above. We are interested in the function of an utterance or part of an utterance in the discourse and thus the sort of questions we ask about an utterance are whether it is intended to evoke a response, whether it is a response itself, whether it is intended to mark a boundary in the discourse, and so on. These concepts will be further explained and exemplified in Chapter 3.

CLASSROOM INTERACTION

Since the late 1940's there has been a growing interest in studies of language interaction inside the classroom. Naturally such studies have had educational priorities and have varied in the degree to which they have related their analytical categories to the linguistic data. Gallagher and Ashner (1963) and Taba *et al.* (1964) both focused on thinking, defined as 'an active transaction between the individual and the demands of his environment, which is neither fully controlled by environmental stimulation, nor wholly independent of some mediating interaction'. Their categories are attempts to analyse one of the purposes of the interaction but are several stages removed from the linguistic data and cannot be directly related to it.

Flanders (1960) focused on what teachers say inside the classroom and the consequences for pupil achievement and involvement. Flanders' system has been used in literally hundreds of independent studies, and also been criticized from a number of different viewpoints. For us the system was not sufficiently consistent; some of the categories were closely related to the linguistic data—Asking Questions, Lecturing, Giving Directions —while others were of a different kind and at a different level of abstraction—Accepting Feeling, Praising or Encouraging, Criticizing or Justifying Authority. Thus while some categories have a direct grammatical realization and discourse function, for others it is much harder to provide an explicit realization.

The work of Barnes (1969) is illuminating. He makes detailed and interesting observations on the kinds of questions teachers ask and the way in which these constrain pupils' thinking and participation. Formally, his work differs from that discussed above in that he does not set out to characterize or analyse all the language in the classroom but simply those aspects which he has found to be interesting and relevant. While accepting that such an approach could produce important and useful findings it was not one we could follow. Our aim was to produce a descriptive system which has the following four minimum criteria, as outlined in Sinclair (1973):

A. The descriptive apparatus should be finite, or else one is not saying anything at all, and may be merely creating the illusion of classification. To take a concrete example, if someone has a pile of objects in front of him and says

This is a wonk, this is a dibble . . .

we do not know what is happening. Perhaps he is giving us the equivalent labels in another language; we have no idea what will be said next. If, however, he begins

> I am going to show you how all objects can be put into one of two classes. This is a wonk, this is a dibble . . .

we know a tremendous amount more. We can predict the next utterance except for the simple choice of *wonk* or *dibble* and we shall have even had some guidance in guessing that.

B. The symbols or terms in the descriptive apparatus should be precisely relatable to their exponents in the data, or else it is not clear what one is saying. If we call some phenomenon a 'noun', or a 'repair strategy' or a 'retreat', we must establish exactly what constitutes the class with that label. The label itself is negligible—it is the criteria which matter. If for example we are told

> Anything with a right angle in it is a wonk. Everything else is a dibble . . .

we don't need any more. The number of classes and the criteria are provided, and off we go. The classification is replicable and clear. There will be problems of interpretation, marginal choices, etc., but that is a feature of all practical classification.

C. The whole of the data should be describable; the descriptive system should be comprehensive. This is not a difficult criterion to meet, because it is always possible to have a 'ragbag' category into which go all items not positively classified by other criteria. But the exercise of building it in is a valuable check on the rest of the description. For example, if we find that 95% of the text goes into the ragbag, we would reject the description as invalid for the text as a whole. If we feel uneasy about putting certain items together in the ragbag, this may well lead to insights later on.

D. There must be at least one impossible combination of symbols. This is the basic notion of linguistic structure, although here couched as a prohibition. A, B, and C above could be general standards for linear string analysis, but this one is linguistic. Language, it seems, never exhausts the possibilities in its structure, thus leaving elbow-room

16

for two major features: style and change. So if a descriptive system of wonks (w) and dibbles (d) allows all two-symbol structures (*ww, dd, wd, dw*) then it is worth looking at three-symbol structures, perhaps to find only *wwd, wdd, dwd, ddd*. It is now clear that no three-symbol string can end in *w*, and we have made a structural statement.

There will probably be all sorts of limitations on four-symbol strings and above, but at the very least we can say that a descriptive apparatus which does not meet this criterion is certainly not showing anything of the structure of what it is describing.

The descriptive system devised by Bellack *et al.* (1966) fits criteria A, C and D, but we did not at first appreciate its relevance. While pursuing educational aims Bellack had progressed a considerable way towards the kind of functional and structural analysis of discourse we were seeking, but he was not working within a linguistic framework.

Bellack proposed a hierarchical structure for lessons with four units, *game*, *sub-game*, *cycle*, and *move*, arranged in a 'consists of' relation. While the two higher units were pedagogically defined the two lower units were defined in discourse terms. The lowest unit, move, is sub-divided into four types, Soliciting, Responding, Structuring, and Reacting, each of which has a different discourse function. They are defined as follows:

Soliciting Moves in this category are intended to elicit (a) an active verbal response on the part of the persons addressed; (b) a cognitive response, e.g. encouraging persons addressed to attend to something; (c) a physical response. All questions are solicitations, as are commands, imperatives and requests.
Responding These moves bear a reciprocal relationship to soliciting moves and occur only in relation to them. Their pedagogical function is to fulfil the expectation of soliciting moves; thus students' answers to teachers' questions are classified as responding moves.
Structuring Structuring moves serve the pedagogical function of setting the context for subsequent behaviour by either launching or halting-excluding interaction between students and teachers. For example, teachers frequently launch a class period with a structuring move in which they focus attention on the topic or problem to be discussed during that session.

Reacting These moves are occasioned by a structuring, soliciting, responding, or prior reacting move, but are not directly elicited by them. Pedagogically, these moves serve to modify (by clarifying, synthesizing, or expanding) and/or to rate (positively or negatively) what has been said previously. Reacting moves differ from responding moves: while a responding move is always directly elicited by a solicitation, preceding moves serve only as the occasion for reactions. (p. 4)

Moves combine together to form cycles. A cycle begins with a structuring or soliciting move and contains one or more responding and reacting moves and continues until the next structuring or soliciting move which initiates a new cycle. One can see here a rudimentary description of the structure of discourse. Of course there are shortcomings. Some parts of teacher utterances do not fit satisfactorily into any of the moves and the reacting category collects everything that does not fit into the other three, but the system does represent a major advance and an encouraging one.

3 THE SYSTEM OF ANALYSIS

This has been a difficult chapter to write because we are catering for two audiences. Most readers will be interested in the broad outlines of the system: what the basic assumptions and premises are, how the various units are defined and related. There will, however, be a few who will want to use the system in their own research work, and for whom this chapter will have to act as a coding manual; they will require much more detail.

To satisfy both requirements, therefore, we felt that it would be helpful to begin with an account of how the system developed, showing the kinds of problem we faced and the decisions we took. We then provide a summary of the system in its present form (pages 28–30) and follow this with definitions of the units and examples of their occurrence in texts.

THE DEVELOPMENT OF THE SYSTEM

When we began we had no preconceptions about the organization or extent of linguistic patterning in long texts. Obviously lessons are highly structured but our problem was to discover how much of this structure was pedagogical and how much linguistic. It seemed possible that the presence of a linguistic introduction was a clue to the boundary of a linguistic unit, but we quickly realized that this is not a useful criterion. On the first morning of the session a headmaster may greet the new intake, 'Good morning children. Welcome to Waseley. This is an important day for you . . .', introducing them to several years of schooling. When the children go to their form-master he also welcomes them and explains their timetables. They go to their first subject lesson. Here the teacher perhaps introduces his subject and goes on to delimit part of it. 'This year we are going to study world geography, starting with the continent of Africa . . . Today I want to look at the rivers of Africa. Let's start with the map. Now, let's see if we can find the main rivers and learn their names—can *you* tell us the name of one river, any one.'

Everything the headmaster and teachers have said so far could be considered as introductions to a series of hierarchically-ordered *units*: the whole of the child's secondary education; a year's work; one subject; a section of that subject; a period or so's work; a part of that period; and a small interactive episode with one pupil. Indeed, in Bellack's system the discourse so far would consist of a series of structuring moves. However, while the language of introduction to each unit is potentially distinctive, despite overlap, we would not want to suggest that for instance 'a year's work' has any linguistic structure. The majority of the units we recognized above are pedagogic ones. To avoid the danger of confusing pedagogic with linguistic structure we determined to work upwards from the smallest linguistic unit. The research problem with contiguous utterances is primarily a descriptive one; major theoretical problems arise when more extensive units are postulated.

We decided to use a rank scale for our descriptive model because of its flexibility. The major advantage of describing new data with a rank scale is that no rank has any more importance than any other and thus if, as we did, one discovers new patterning it is a fairly simple process to create a new rank to handle it. There is, of course, the ever-present temptation of creating new ranks to cope with every little problem (see Chapter 5 for further discussion).

The basic assumption of a rank scale is that a unit at a given rank, for example, *word*, is made up of one or more units of the rank below, *morphemes*, and combines with other units at the same rank to make one unit at the rank above, *group* (Halliday 1961). The unit at the lowest rank has no structure. For example, in grammar 'morpheme' is the smallest unit, and cannot be subdivided into smaller grammatical units. However, if one moves from the *level* of grammar to the level of phonology, morphemes can be shown to be composed of a series of phonemes. Similarly, the smallest unit at the level of discourse will have no structure, although it is composed of words, groups or clauses at the level of grammar.

Each rank above the lowest has a structure which can be expressed in terms of the units next below. Thus, the structure of a clause can be expressed in terms of nominal, verbal, adverbial, and prepositional groups. The unit at the highest rank is one which has a structure that can be expressed in terms of lower units, but does not itself form part of the structure of any higher unit. It is for this reason that 'sentence' is regarded as the highest unit of grammar. Paragraphs have no grammatical structure; they consist of a series of sentences of any type in any order. Where there are no grammatical constraints on what an individual can do, variations are often dubbed 'stylistic'.

We assumed that when, from a linguistic point of view, classroom discourse became an unconstrained string of units, the organization would have become fundamentally pedagogic. While we could then make observations on teacher style, further analysis of structure would require a change of level not rank.

We then looked at adjacent utterances, trying to discover what constituted an appropriate reply to a teacher's question, and how the teacher signalled whether the reply was appropriate or inappropriate.

Initially we felt the need for only two ranks, *utterance* and *exchange*; utterance was defined as everything said by one speaker before another began to speak, exchange as two or more utterances. However, we quickly experienced difficulties with these categories. The following example has three utterances, but how many exchanges?

Teacher	Can you tell me why do you eat all that food?
	Yes.
Pupil	To keep you strong.
Teacher	To keep you strong. Yes. To keep you strong.
	Why do you want to be strong? (Text G)

The obvious boundary occurs in the middle of the teacher's second utterance, which suggests that there is a unit smaller than utterance. Following Bellack we called this a *move*, and wondered for a while whether moves combined to form utterances which in turn combined to form exchanges. However, the example above is not an isolated one; the vast majority of exchanges have their boundaries within utterances. Thus, although utterance had many points to recommend it as a unit of discourse, not least ease of definition, we reluctantly abandoned it. We now express the structure of exchanges in terms of moves. A typical exchange in the classroom consists of an *initiation* by the teacher, followed by a *response* from the pupil, followed by *feedback*, to the pupil's response from the teacher, as in the above example. These categories correspond very closely with Bellack's moves, soliciting, responding, and reacting.

While we were looking at exchanges we noticed that a small set of words—'right', 'well', 'good', 'O.K.', 'now', recurred frequently in the speech of all teachers. We realized that these

21

words functioned to indicate boundaries in the lesson, the end of one stage and the beginning of the next. Silverman (1972) notes their occurrence in job interviews and Pearce (1973) in broadcast interviews where the function is exactly the same. We labelled them *frame*. Teachers vary in the particular word they favour but a frame occurs invariably at the beginning of a lesson, marking off the settling-down time.

Now,
I want to tell you about a King who lived a long time ago in Ancient Egypt.   (Text B)

Well,
today, erm, I thought we'd do three quizzes.   (Text D)

An example of a frame within a lesson is:

> Energy. Yes.
> When you put petrol in the car you're putting another kind of energy in the car from the petrol. So we get energy from petrol and we get energy from food. Two kinds of energy.

Frame   *Now then*
> I want you to take your pen and rub it as hard as you can on something woollen.   (Text G)

We then observed that frames, especially those at the beginning of a lesson, are frequently followed by a special kind of statement, the function of which is to tell the class what is going to happen (see the examples from Texts B and D above). These items are not strictly part of the discourse, but rather metastatements about the discourse—we call them *focus*, and these correspond very closely with Bellack's structuring moves. The boundary elements, frame and focus, were the first positive evidence of the existence of a unit above exchange, which we later labelled *transaction*.

We have isolated a large number of exchange types with unique structures; exchanges combine to form transactions and it seems probable that there will also be a number of transaction types—concerned mainly with giving information, or directing pupil activity, or question-and-answer routines—but we cannot isolate them yet. The unanswered question is whether we will be able to provide structures for transactions or whether the way exchanges are combined to form transactions will prove to be purely a feature of teacher style.

The highest unit of classroom discourse, consisting of one or more transactions, we call *lesson*. This unit may frequently be co-extensive with the pedagogical unit *period*, but need not be.

For several months we continued using these four ranks—move, exchange, transaction, lesson—but found that we were experiencing difficulty coding at the lowest rank. For example, to code the following as simply an initiation seemed inadequate.

Now I'm going to show you a word and I want you—anyone who can—to tell me if they can tell me what the word says. Now it's a bit difficult. It's upside down for some of you isn't it? Anyone think they know what it says?

(Hands raised)

Two people. Three people. Lets see what you think, Martin, what do you think it says?

We then realized that moves were structured and so we needed another rank with which we could describe their structure. This we called *act*.

Acts and moves in discourse are very similar to morphemes and words in grammar. By definition, move is the smallest free unit although it has a structure in terms of acts. Just as there are bound morphemes which cannot alone realize words, so there are bound acts which cannot alone realize moves.

We need to distinguish discourse acts from grammatical structures, or there would be no point in proposing a new level of language description—we would simply be analysing the higher ranks of grammar. Of course if acts did turn out to be arrangements of clauses in a consistent and hierarchical fashion, then they would replace (in speech) our confusing notions of 'sentence' and the higher ranks of what we now call discourse would arrange themselves on top.

The evidence is not conclusive and we need comparative data from other types of discourse. We would argue, however, for a separate level of discourse because, as we show in detail later, grammatical structure is not sufficient to determine which discourse act a particular grammatical unit realizes—one needs to take account of both relevant situational information and position in the discourse.

The lowest rank of the discourse scale overlaps with the top of the grammar scale (see figure 1). Discourse acts are typically one free clause, plus any subordinate clauses, but there are certain closed classes where we can specify almost all the possible realizations which consist of single words or groups.

Figure 1 Levels and ranks

Non-Linguistic Organization	DISCOURSE	Grammar
course		
period	LESSON	
topic	TRANSACTION	
	EXCHANGE	
	MOVE	sentence
	ACT	clause
		group
		word
		morpheme

There is a similar overlap at the top of the discourse scale. We have been constantly aware of the danger of creating a rank for which there is only pedagogical evidence. We have deliberately chosen *lesson*, a word specific to the particular language situation we are investigating, as the label for the top rank. We feel fairly certain that the four lower ranks will be present in other discourse; the fifth may also be, in which case, once we have studied comparative data, we will use a more general label.

We see the level of discourse as lying between the level of *grammar* and *non-linguistic organization*. There is no need to suppose a one-to-one correspondence of units between levels; the levels of phonology and grammar overlap considerably, but have only broad general correspondence. We see the top of our discourse scale, lesson, corresponding roughly to the rank *period* in the non-linguistic level, and the bottom of our scale, *act*, corresponding roughly to the clause complex in grammar.

SUMMARY OF THE SYSTEM OF ANALYSIS

This research has been very much text-based. We began with very few preconceptions and the descriptive system has grown and been modified to cope with problems thrown up by the data. The system we have produced is hierarchical and our method of presentation is closely modelled on Halliday's *Categories of a Theory of Grammar*. All the terms used—structure, system, rank, level, delicacy, realization, marked, unmarked—are Halliday's. To permit readers to gain an over-all impression, the whole system is first presented at primary delicacy and then given a much more discursive treatment.

Working downwards, each rank is first named. Then the elements of structure are named, and the structure is stated in a general way, using shortened forms of the names of elements. Brackets indicate options.

The link between one rank and the next below is through *classes*. A class realizes an element of structure, and in this summary classes are both numbered and named.

Let us look at one of the tables as an example:

RANK II: Transaction

Elements of Structure	Structures	Classes of Exchange
Preliminary (P) Medial (M) Terminal (T)	PM $(M^2 \ldots M^n)$ (T)	P, T: Boundary (II.1) M: Teaching (II.2)

This table identifies the rank as second from the top of the scale, i.e. transaction. It states that there are three elements of structure, called *Preliminary* (short symbol P), *Medial* (M), and *Terminal* (T). In the next column is given a composite statement of the possible structures of this transaction—PM $(M^2 \ldots M^n)$ (T). Anything within brackets is optional, so this formula states:

a) there must be a preliminary move in each transaction,
b) there must be one medial move, but there may be any number of them,
c) there can be a terminal move, but not necessarily.

In the third column the elements of transaction structure are associated with the classes of the rank next below (exchange), because each element is realized by a class of exchange. Preliminary and terminal exchange, it is claimed, are selected from the same class of move called *Boundary* moves, and this is numbered for ease of reference. The element medial is realized by a class of exchange called *Teaching*. Later tables develop the structure of these exchanges at rank III.

RANK I: Lesson

Elements of Structure	Structures	Classes
	an unordered series of transactions	

RANK III: Exchange (Boundary)

Elements of Structure	Structures	Classes of Move
Frame (Fr) Focus (Fo)	(Fr) (Fo)	Fr: Framing (III.1) Fo: Focusing (III.2)

RANK III: Exchange (Teaching)

Elements of Structure	Structures	Classes of Move
Initiation (I) Response (R) Feedback (F)	I (R) (F)	I: Opening (III.3) R: Answering (III.4) F: Follow-up (III.5)

RANK IV: Move (Opening)

Elements of Structure	Structures	Classes of Act
signal (s) pre-head (pre-h) head (h) post-head (post-h) select (sel)	(s) (pre-h) h (post-h) (sel) (sel) (pre-h) h	s: marker (IV.1) pre-h: starter (IV.2) h: system operating at h; choice of elicitation, directive, informative, check (IV.3) post-h: system operating at post-h; choice from prompt and clue (IV.4) sel: ((cue) bid) nomination (IV.5)

RANK IV: Move (Answering)

Elements of Structure	Structures	Classes of Act
pre-head (pre-h) head (h) post-head (post-h)	(pre-h) h (post-h)	pre-h: acknowledge (IV.6) h: system operating at h; choice of reply, react, acknowledge (IV.7) post-h: comment (IV.8)

RANK IV: Move (Follow-up)

Elements of Structure	Structures	Classes of Act
pre-head (pre-h) head (h) post-head (post-h)	(pre-h) (h) (post-h)	pre-h: accept (IV.9) h: evaluate (IV.10) post-h: comment (IV.8)

RANK IV: Move (Framing)

Elements of Structure	Structures	Classes of Act
head (h) qualifier (q)	hq	h: marker (IV.1) q: silent stress (IV.11)

RANK IV: Move (Focusing)

Elements of Structure	Structures	Classes of Act
signal (s) pre-head (pre-h) head (h) post-head (post-h)	(s) (pre-h) h (post-h)	s: marker (IV.1) pre-h: starter (IV.2) h: system at h; choice from metastatement or conclusion (IV.12) post-h: comment (IV.8)

EXPLANATION OF THE SYSTEM OF ANALYSIS

The previous section presented a downward view showing how units at each rank had structures realized by units at the rank below. This section begins at the lowest rank and discusses the realization and recognition of acts; it then moves on to discuss the structures of moves, exchanges, transactions and lessons.

Acts

The units at the lowest rank of discourse are *acts* and correspond most nearly to the grammatical unit *clause*, but when we describe an item as an act we are doing something very different from when we describe it as a clause. Grammar is concerned with the *formal* properties of an item, discourse with the *functional*

27

properties, with what the speaker is using the item for. The four sentence types, declarative, interrogative, imperative, and moodless, realize twenty-one discourse acts, many of them specialized and some quite probably classroom-specific.

There are three major acts which probably occur in all forms of spoken discourse—*elicitation*, *directive*, and *informative*—and they appear in classroom discourse as the heads of *Initiating moves*. An elicitation is an act the function of which is to request a linguistic response—linguistic, although the response may be a non-verbal surrogate such as a nod or raised hand. A directive is an act the function of which is to request a non-linguistic response is simply an acknowledgement that one is listening.
ing at the blackboard, writing, listening. An informative is as the name suggests, an act whose function is to pass on ideas, facts, opinions, information and to which the appropriate response is simply an acknowledgment that one is listening.

Elicitations, directives and informatives are very frequently realized by interrogatives, imperatives, and declaratives respectively, but there are occasions when this is not so. A native speaker who interpreted 'Is that the mint-sauce over there?' or 'Can you tell me the time?' as yes/no questions, 'Have a drink' as a command, or 'I wish you'd go away' as requiring just a murmur of agreement, would find the world a bewildering place full of irritable people. These are examples of the contrast which can occur between form and function.

The opportunity for variety arises from the relationship between grammar and discourse. The *unmarked* form of a directive may be imperative, 'Shut the door', but there are many *marked* versions, using interrogative, declarative, and moodless structures.

> can you shut the door
> would you mind shutting the door
> I wonder if you could shut the door
> the door is still open
> the door

To handle this lack of fit between grammar and discourse we suggest two intermediate areas where distinctive choices can be postulated: situation and tactics. Both of these terms already have various meanings in linguistics but still seem appropriate to our purpose. *Situation* here includes all relevant factors in the environment, social conventions, and the shared experience of the participants. The criterion of relevance is obviously vague and ill-defined at the moment though some dignity can be attached to it on the grounds that anyone who considers such factors irrelevant must arrive at a different interpretation of the discourse. Examples of situational features 'considered relevant' and the use to which they are put in the analysis of classroom language will be detailed below.

The other area of distinctive choice, *tactics*, handles the syntagmatic patterns of discourse: the way in which items precede, follow and are related to each other. It is place in the structure of the discourse which finally determines which act a particular grammatical item is realizing, though classification can only be made of items already tagged with features from grammar and situation.

Situation

In situation we use, at present in an *ad hoc* and unsystematized way, knowledge about schools, classrooms, one particular moment in a lesson, to reclassify items already labelled by the grammar. Usually the grammatical types declarative, interrogative, imperative, realize the situational categories *statement*, *question, command*, but this is not always so. Of the nine possible combinations—declarative statement, declarative question, declarative command, and so on—there is only one we cannot instance: imperative statement.

For ease of reference the situational and grammatical categories are listed in the table below, together with their discourse category equivalents.

discourse categories	situational categories	grammatical categories
informative elicitation directive	statement question command	declarative interrogative imperative

The interrogative, 'What are you laughing at?', is interpretable either as a question, or as a command to stop laughing. Inside the classroom it is usually the latter. In one of our tapes a teacher plays a recording of a television programme in which there is a psychologist with a 'posh' accent. The teacher wants to explore the children's attitude to accent and the value

29

judgements they base on it. When the recording is finished the teacher begins,

Teacher   What kind of a person do you think he is? Do you—what are you laughing at?

Pupil   Nothing.   (Text F)

The pupil interpreted the teacher's interrogative as a directive to stop laughing, but that was not the teacher's intention. He had rejected his first question because he realized that the pupil's laughter was an indication of her attitude, and if he could get her to explain why she was laughing he would have an excellent opening to the topic. He continues and the pupil realizes her mistake.

Teacher   Pardon?
Pupil   Nothing.
Teacher   You're laughing at nothing, nothing at all?
Pupil   No.
           It's funny really 'cos they don't think as though they were there they might not like it. And it sounds rather a pompous attitude.

The girl's mistake lay in misunderstanding the situation not the sentence, and the example demonstrates the crucial role of situation in the analysis of discourse. We can at the moment make only a rudimentary attempt to deal with situation. We suggest four questions one can ask about the situation and depending on the answers to these questions and the grammatical form of the clause, propose three rules which predict the correct interpretation of teacher utterances most of the time. The questions we ask are

1. If the clause is interrogative is the addressee also the subject?
2. What actions or activities are physically possible at the time of utterance?
3. What actions or activities are proscribed at the time of utterance?
4. What actions or activities have been prescribed up to the time of utterance?

Using the answers to these questions we can formulate three rules to predict when a declarative or interrogative will be realizing something other than a statement or question. See figure 2 for a systemic treatment of the classification of interrogatives by means of these rules.

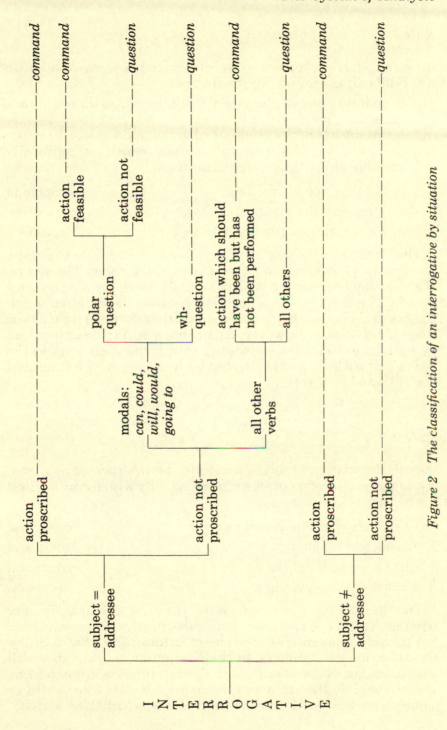

Figure 2 The classification of an interrogative by situation

31

Rule 1

An interrogative clause is to be interpreted as a *command to do* if it fulfils all the following conditions:

 (i) it contains one of the modals *can, could, will, would* (and sometimes *going to*);

 (ii) if the subject of the clause is also the addressee;

(iii) the predicate describes an action which is physically possible at the time of the utterance.

1. can you play the piano, John	command
2. can John play the piano	question
3. can you swim a length, John	question

The first example is a command because it fulfils the three conditions—assuming there is a piano in the room. The second is a question because the subject and addressee are not the same person. The third is also a question because the children are in the classroom, and the activity is not therefore possible at the time of utterance. However, as we have so far discovered no exceptions to this rule, we predict that if the class were at the swimming baths example 3 would be interpreted as a command and followed by a splash.

Rule 2

Any declarative or interrogative is to be interpreted as a *command to stop* if it refers to an action or activity which is proscribed at the time of the utterance.

1. I can hear someone laughing	command
2. is someone laughing	command
3. what are you laughing at	command
4. what are you laughing at	question

The declarative command, as in the first example, is very popular with some teachers. It is superficially an observation, but its only relevance at the time of utterance is that it draws the attention of 'someone' to their laughter, so that they will stop laughing. Examples 2 and 3, though interrogative in form, work in exactly the same way. Example 4 is only interpreted as a question when laughter is not regarded as a forbidden activity.

32

Rule 3

Any declarative or interrogative is to be interpreted as *command to do* if it refers to an action or activity which teacher and pupil(s) know ought to have been performed or completed and hasn't been.

1. the door is still open	command
2. did you shut the door	command
3. did you shut the door	question

Example 1 states a fact which all relevant participants already know; example 2 is apparently a question to which all participants know the answer. Both serve to draw attention to what hasn't been done in order to cause someone to do it. Example 3 is a question only when the teacher does *not* know whether the action has been performed.

Labov (1970) independently proposes a rule for the interpretation of questions in conversation which is very close to rule 3 above.

If A makes a request for information of B about whether an action X has been performed, or at what time T, X will be performed, and the four preconditions below hold, then A will be heard as making an underlying form 'B: do X!'

The preconditions are, that A believes that B believes:

1. X should be done for a purpose Y.
2. B has the ability to do X.
3. B has the obligation to do X.
4. A has the right to tell B to do X.

For us, preconditions 1, 3, and 4 are part of the general teaching situation and do not need to be invoked for the interpretation of a particular utterance.

Tactics

In *grammar* we classify an item by its structure; from the relative position of subject and verb we label a clause declarative, interrogative or imperative. In *situation* we use information about the non-linguistic environment to reclassify items as statement, question or command. We need to know what has happened so far in the classroom, what the classroom contains, what the atmosphere is like, but given such detailed information we can make a situational classification of even an isolated clause. However, the *discourse* value of an item depends on what linguistic items have preceded it, what are expected to follow and what do follow. We handle such sequence relationships in *tactics*.

The definitions of the discourse acts, informative, elicitation, and directive, make them sound remarkably similar to statement, question, and command but there are major differences. While elicitations are always realized by questions, directives by commands, and informatives by statements, the relationship is not reciprocal: questions can realize many other acts and the expression 'rhetorical question' is a recognition of this fact. Statements, questions and commands are only informatives, elicitations and directives when they are initiating; an elicitation is an initiating question of which the function is to gain a verbal response from another speaker—questions occur at many other places in the discourse but then their function is different, and this must be stressed. A question which is not intended to get a reply is realizing a different act from one which is; the speaker is using the question for a different purpose and we must recognize this in our description.

Spoken discourse is produced in real time and our descriptive system attempts to deal with the 'now-coding' aspect of speech. Speakers inevitably make mistakes, or realize that they could have expressed what they intended much better. A teacher may produce a question which he fully intends as an elicitation and then change his mind. Obviously he can't erase what he has said, and he doesn't tell the children to ignore it, but he does signal that the children are not expected to respond as if it were an elicitation. In the 'what are you laughing at' example discussed above, the teacher abruptly changes course in the middle of a question. This is rare and signals to the class that what has gone before should be regarded as if it had never been said, should be deleted completely. More frequently, as in the example below, the teacher follows one potential informative, directive or elicitation with another, usually more explicit one, signalling paralinguistically, by intonation, absence of pausing, speeding up his speech rate, that he now considers what he has just said a *starter*, and the pupils are not intended to respond. Starters are acts of which the function is to provide information about, or direct attention or thought towards, an area in order to make a correct response to the initiation more likely, even though this function is often only impromptu, when the teacher realizes that the intended elicitation was not adequate. What he has said can, however, serve as a starter to get the children thinking in the right area, and then the more explicit elicitation has more chance of success.

1. T   *What about this one? This I think is a super one.* Isobel, can you think what it means?

2. P   Does it mean there's been an accident further along the road?

3. T   No.

4. P   Does it mean a double bend ahead?

5. T   No, look at the car. (tilts picture)

6. P   Slippery roads?

7. T   Yes. It means be careful because the road's very slippery.
                                              (Text D)

The teacher begins with a question which appears to have been intended as an elicitation. She changes her mind and relegates it to a starter. The following statement is in turn relegated by a second question which then does stand as an elicitation.

To recap: while speaking the teacher produces a series of clauses classifiable as statements, questions and commands in *situation*. If the teacher then allows a pupil to speak, these clauses are seen as initiating, and have the discourse value of informative elicitation, directive; if he follows one of these clauses with another it is pushed down to act as a starter.

In any succession of statements, questions, and commands the pupil knows that he usually only has to respond to the final one, and only that has an initiating function. This can lead to an incorrect response if the pupil doesn't fully understand what the teacher is saying. In the following example a quoted question is understood as an elicitation.

Pupil   Well, he should take some look at what the man's point of view is.

Teacher   Yes, yes.

But he wasn't asked that question don't forget. He was merely asked the question 'Why, why are they reacting like this?'

Pupil   Well, maybe its the way they've been brought up.
                                              (Text F)

35

At the head of each initiating move by the teacher is one elicitation, directive, or informative. That is to say, a move constitutes a coherent contribution to the interaction which essentially serves one purpose. The purpose is selected from a very small set of available choices. Where a move is made up of more than one act, the other acts are subsidiary to the one which is the head, and optional in the structure. The teacher's initiation is typically followed by a responding move from a pupil, and the structures here are sufficiently regular for us to identify a regular type of response to each.

$$\text{Initiation} \begin{cases} \text{directive} \longrightarrow \text{(acknowledge) react} \\ \text{informative} \longrightarrow \text{acknowledge} \\ \text{elicitation} \longrightarrow \text{reply} \end{cases}$$

React is the performance of whatever action is required by the directive; *acknowledge*, a verbal or non-verbal signal which confirms that the pupil is listening and understanding. Acknowledge is also an optional part of the response to a directive, when it serves to let the teacher know that the pupil has heard.

John, I wonder if you could open that window.

Yes/mm/sure.

The response to an elicitation is a *reply*. Replies are all too often one word moodless utterances, but they can also be realized by statements, as in text F above, 'Well, he should take some look at what the man's point of view is.'; or questions as in text D above, 'Does it mean a double bend ahead?'.

A reply can optionally be followed by *comment*. Comments serve to exemplify, expand, justify, provide additional information about the head of the move, and can occur in *Follow-up* and *Focusing* moves as well as *Answering* moves. Comments are almost always realized by statements or tag-questions.

Pupil   Are the number for le—for the letters?

Teacher   Yes.
            They're—that's the order, one, two, three, four.   (Text C)

A special feature of the classroom situation is that a number of individuals have (been) gathered together for the specific purpose of learning something. They answer questions and follow instructions and they need to know whether they are performing adequately. A teacher rarely asks a question because he wants to know the answer; he asks a question because he wants to know whether a pupil knows the answer. In such a situation the pupils need to know whether their answer was 'right', and an act we label *evaluate* is of vital importance. If we think of the following exchange

What time is it, Susan?

Three o'clock,

the closing item outside the classroom could well be 'Thanks', inside the classroom, 'Good girl'. In evaluate, the teacher presents his estimation of the pupil's response and creates a basis for proceeding. Evaluate is usually realized by a statement, sometimes by a tag question.

Evaluate is often preceded by *accept*, an act which confirms that the teacher has heard or seen the response and that it was an appropriate one. It is frequently used when a child's reply is wrong, but the teacher wants to encourage the child. There is always the problem that in rejecting a reply one might reject the child. Accept is realized by a closed set consisting of 'yes', 'no', 'fine', 'good', or by a repetition of the reply, which has either a falling intonation, tone 1, or a low rising intonation, tone 3, which suggests that there is another answer.[1] Alternatively, following a pupil's wrong answer, one can get an accepting 'yes' with a fall-rise intonation, tone 4, which leads on to a negative evaluation or a *clue* (see below).

In all forms of spoken discourse there are rules about who speaks when (Schegloff and Sacks 1973). Within the classroom the teacher has the right to speak whenever he wants to, and children contribute to the discourse when he allows them to. Teachers differ in the degree of formality they impose on children's contributions, and the rigidity with which they stick to the rule of 'no shouting out'. As noted above, a typical structure of a classroom exchange is a teacher elicitation followed by a pupil reply. However, a teacher elicitation followed by thirty replies would be useless and most teachers have a way of selecting which pupil will reply. Sometimes teachers *nominate* a child to answer; sometimes children raise their hands or shout 'Miss, Miss', *bidding* to be nominated, to be given permission to speak, and sometimes the teacher gives the children a *cue* to bid, 'hands up'. Cue is a command but not a directive. It is addressed to the class, but they do not all raise their hands because the command is to be interpreted as 'Put your hands up if you know'. We can

[1] A succinct account of the description of intonation used here is given in Halliday (1970).

37

compare this with a real directive, when the whole class is expected to react. In the following extract there are examples of both.

Directive	*All eyes on me.* Put your pencils down. Fold your arms. Hands on your heads. Hands on your shoulders. Hands on your knees. Fold your arms. Look at me.
Cue	*Hands up.* What's that. (Text H)

Nomination, bid, and cue are all subordinate elements of the teacher's initiating move, and there are two other acts which occur in initiating moves—*clue* and *prompt*. Clue is a statement, question, command, or moodless item, subordinate to the head of the initiation which provides additional information to help the pupil answer the elicitation or comply with the directive. 'Look at the car', in the example from Text D quoted above, is a clue. It does not have the status of a directive because its function is not to cause a pupil reaction. If the whole class simply looked at the car the teacher would be very annoyed; the children are to look at the car in the light of the elicitation 'Can you think what it means?'. Another example of a clue, here realized by a statement, is

Teacher	What does the petrol change to?
Pupils	Smoke.
	Water.
	Fire.
Teacher	*You told me before.* (Text G)

Sometimes elicitations or directives are reinforced by another act, *prompt*. We said above that elicitations and directives request a response; a prompt suggests that the teacher is not requesting but expecting or even demanding. Prompts are always realized by commands, and a closed set at that. The ones we have discovered so far are 'go on', 'come on', 'hurry up', 'quickly', 'have a guess'.

There are four more acts to introduce: *marker, metastatement, conclusion, loop*. Marker is an item whose sole function is to indicate a boundary in the discourse. It is realized by a very small set of words, 'well', 'O.K.', 'right', 'now', 'good', 'all right', and can occur at the beginning of opening, focusing and framing moves.

Metastatement is an act occurring in a focusing move, whose

function is to state what the discourse is going to be about. In other words it is technically not part of the discourse but a commentary on the discourse. Such items are not informatives because the teacher is not telling the children something, he is telling them what he is going to tell them. Thus,

Now, *I want to tell you about a king who lived a long time ago.* . . . (Text B)

Conclusion is a special kind of statement which occurs at the end of some transactions and summarizes what has been done. In a way it is the converse of metastatement. Conclusions are marked by 'so' or 'then', and often also a noticeable slowing in rate of speech.

So that then is why the Pharaohs built their pyramids.   (Text C)

Right. *So that's the first quiz.*   (Text D)

Sometimes the channel of communication is too noisy and the teacher needs the child to repeat what he has just said. The act he uses we call *loop*; it is realized by 'pardon', 'you what', 'eh', 'again', and functions to take the discourse back to the stage it was at before the pupil spoke. The channel noise cannot be only one-way, but it is significant that no child in any of our tapes ever admits to not having heard something the teacher has said. Thus, we only have examples of teacher loops. Loop can of course be used tactically to draw the attention of the class to something one child has said.

Teacher	You told me before.
Pupil	Energy.
Teacher	*Again.*
Pupil	Energy. (Text G)

There are a number of speech acts that are not specifically part of the discourse. We refer to these as *asides*. They include remarks by the teacher which are unrelated to the discourse, though not to the situation. Often they are muttered under the breath.

It's freezing in here.   (Text C)

The Egyptians, and—
when I can find my chart. Here it is—
Here are some of the symbols they used.   (Text D)

39

The classes of acts

There now follows a summary of all the acts, each numbered as they were in the summary of analysis on pages 25–7. First the name, then the symbol used in coding, then the functional definition and characteristic formal features. For the closed class items there is a list of all the examples so far discovered.

Reference Number	*Label*	*Symbol*	*Realization and Definition*
IV.1	marker	m	Realized by a closed class of items—'well', 'O.K.', 'now', 'good', 'right', 'alright'. When a marker is acting as the head of a framing move it has a falling intonation, [1] or [1+], as well as silent stress. Its function is to mark boundaries in the discourse.
IV.2	starter	s	Realized by statement, question or command. Its function is to provide information about or direct attention to or thought towards an area in order to make a correct response to the initiation more likely.
IV.3.1	elicitation	el	Realized by question. Its function is to request a linguistic response.
IV.3.2	check	ch	Realized by a closed class of polar questions concerned with being 'finished' or 'ready', having 'problems' or 'difficulties', being able to 'see' or 'hear'. They are 'real' questions, in that for once the teacher doesn't know the answer. If he does know the answer to, for example, 'have you finished', it is a directive, not a check. The function of checks is to enable the teacher to ascertain whether there are any problems preventing the successful progress of the lesson.

IV.3.3	directive	d	Realized by imperative. Its function is to request a non-linguistic response.
IV.3.4	informative	i	Realized by statement. It differs from other uses of statement in that its sole function is to provide information. The only response is an acknowledgement of attention and understanding.
IV.4.1	prompt	p	Realized by a closed class of items—'go on', 'come on', 'hurry up', 'quickly', 'have a guess'. Its function is to reinforce a directive or elicitation by suggesting that the teacher is no longer requesting a response but expecting or even demanding one.
IV.4.2	clue	cl	Realized by statement, question, command, or moodless item. It is subordinate to the head of the initiation and functions by providing additional information which helps the pupil to answer the elicitation or comply with the directive.
IV.5.1	cue	cu	Realized by a closed class of which we have only three exponents, 'hands up', 'don't call out', 'is John the only one'. Its sole function is to evoke an (appropriate) bid.
IV.5.2	bid	b	Realized by a closed class of verbal and non-verbal items—'Sir', 'Miss', teacher's name, raised hand, heavy breathing, finger clicking. Its function is to signal a desire to contribute to the discourse.

Reference Number	Label	Symbol	Realization and Definition
IV.5.3	nomination	n	Realized by a closed class consisting of the names of all the pupils, 'you' with contrastive stress, 'anybody', 'yes', and one or two idiosyncratic items such as 'who hasn't said anything yet'. The function of nomination is to call on or give permission to a pupil to contribute to the discourse.
IV.6	acknowledge	ack	Realized by 'yes', 'O.K.', 'cor', 'mm', 'wow', and certain non-verbal gestures and expressions. Its function is simply to show that the initiation has been understood, and, if the head was a directive, that the pupil intends to react.
IV.7.1	reply	rep	Realized by statement, question, moodless and non-verbal surrogates such as nods. Its function is to provide a linguistic response which is appropriate to the elicitation.
IV.7.2	react	rea	Realized by a non-linguistic action. Its function is to provide the appropriate non-linguistic response defined by the preceding directive.
IV.8	comment	com	Realized by statement and tag question. It is subordinate to the head of the move and its function is to exemplify, expand, justify, provide additional information. On the written page it is difficult to distinguish from informative because the outsider's ideas of relevance are not always the same. However, teachers signal paralinguistically, by a pause, when they are beginning a new initiation with an informative as a head; otherwise they see themselves as commenting.

IV.9	accept	acc	Realized by a closed class of items—'yes', 'no', 'good', 'fine', and repetition of pupil's reply, all with neutral low fall intonation. Its function is to indicate that the teacher has heard or seen and that the informative, reply or react was appropriate.
IV.10	evaluate	e	Realized by statements and tag questions including words and phrases such as 'good', 'interesting', 'team point', commenting on the quality of the reply, react or initiation, also by 'yes', 'no', 'good', 'fine', with a high fall intonation, and repetition of the pupil's reply with either high fall, (positive), or a rise of any kind, (negative evaluation).
IV.11	silent stress	^	Realized by a pause, of the duration of one or more beats, following a marker. It functions to highlight the marker when it is serving as the head of a boundary exchange indicating a transaction boundary.
IV.12.1	meta-statement	ms	Realized by a statement which refers to some future time when what is described will occur. Its function is to help the pupils to see the structure of the lesson, to help them understand the purpose of the subsequent exchange, and see where they are going.
IV.12.2	conclusion	con	Realized by an anaphoric statement, sometimes marked by slowing of speech rate and usually the lexical items 'so' or 'then'. In a way it is the converse of metastatement. Its function is again to help the pupils understand the structure of the lesson but this time by summarizing what the preceding chunk of discourse was about.

43

Reference Number	Label	Symbol	Realization and Definition
IV.13	loop	l	Realized by a closed class of items—'pardon', 'you what', 'eh', 'again', with rising intonation and a few questions like 'did you say', 'do you mean'. Its function is to return the discourse to the stage it was at before the pupil spoke, from where it can proceed normally.
IV.14	aside	z	Realized by statement, question, command, moodless, usually marked by lowering the tone of the voice, and not really addressed to the class. As we noted above, this category covers items we have difficulty in dealing with. It is really instances of the teacher talking to himself, 'It's freezing in here', 'Where did I put my chalk?'

The structure and classes of moves

Moves are made up of acts, and moves themselves occupy places in the structure of exchanges. In this account the structure of moves is described class by class. By referring to the tables on pages 25–7 it will be seen that there are five classes of move and that these realize two classes of exchange—*Boundary* and *Teaching*. *Framing* and *Focusing* moves realize boundary exchanges and *Opening*, *Answering*, and *Follow-up* moves realize teaching exchanges.

Each of these moves has a different function. Framing moves are indications by the teacher that he regards one stage in the lesson as ended and that another is beginning. Framing moves are probably a feature of all spoken discourse—shop assistants often use them to indicate that they have finished serving one customer and are ready for the next—but occur more frequently in classroom language because it is carefully structured by one participant. Framing moves are realized by a marker followed by silent stress, 'Right∧'.

Framing moves are frequently, though not always, followed

by focusing moves the function of which is to talk about the discourse, to tell the children what is going to happen or what has happened. Focusing moves represent a change of plane. The teacher stands for a moment outside the discourse and says 'We are going to/have been communicating; this is what our communication will be/was about'. Focusing moves have an optional marker and starter, a compulsory head, realized by a metastatement or a conclusion, and an optional comment. In the examples which follow, the third column contains the structural label of the item, the fourth column the label of the act which occurs at that place in the structure.

Classes of move			Structure of move	Classes of act
Framing	Right	^	h q	marker silent stress
Focusing	Now, what we've just done, what we've just done is given some energy to this pen.		s h	marker conclusion

(Text G)

With focusing moves, as with many units in discourse, there are possible ambiguities, and the teacher who focuses 'Today we are going to play rounders' must be careful to continue quickly 'but first we must finish our sums', or the children might interpret his focus as an opening move and bound out of the classroom.

The function of an opening move is to cause others to participate in an exchange. Opening and answering are complementary moves. The purpose of a given opening may be passing on information or directing an action or eliciting a fact. The type of answering move is predetermined because its function is to be an appropriate response in the terms laid down by the opening move.

The structure we provide for opening moves is complicated. Much of this complexity arises from the element *select* which is where the teacher chooses which pupil he wants to respond. Select can be realized by a simple teacher nomination, or by a pupil bid followed by a nomination, or by a teacher cue followed by a bid and a nomination.

45

It would be possible to suggest that teaching exchanges actually have a structure of five moves, with both bid and nomination as separate moves. The argument for this would be that a new move should begin every time there is a change of speaker. We rejected this alternative, because it would have created as many difficulties as it would have solved. When a teacher nominated without waiting for a bid, we would have had to regard this as two moves, one consisting of a single word, and at times even embedded inside the other move. Such a solution would also have devalued the concept of move. We prefer to say that a move boundary signals a change in the speaker who is composing/creating the discourse, and therefore that a move boundary is a potential change in the direction of the discourse, whereas a child making a bid must choose from a very limited set of choices. Thus we regard the function of an opening move, with elicitation or directive as head, as not only requesting a reply or reaction but as also deciding who should respond. An opening move ends after the responder has been selected.

Prompt and clue can also occur in a post-head position in opening moves. This means that the structure of a teacher's opening move is,

(signal) (pre-head) head (post-head) (select)

with brackets showing that all elements except head are optional. The example below has all the elements except *signal*.

Classes of move		Structure of move	Classes of act
Opening	A group of people used symbols to do their writing. They used pictures instead of as we write in words.	pre-h	starter
	Do you know who those people were?	h	elicitation
	I'm sure you do.	post-h	prompt
	Joan.	sel	nomination

(Text D)

Pupil opening moves have a simpler structure. There are no examples of signal; pre-heads can, but rarely do, occur; post-

heads, realized by prompt and clue, by their very nature are not the sort of acts used by pupils. As the pupil must indicate that he wants to speak, *select* ocurs before the head. Sometimes the teacher will allow the pupil to follow his bid with an elicitation or informative, sometimes he insists on the nomination. We must emphasize that the pupil has no right to contribute to the discourse, and the teacher can ignore him. In the following example the pupil thinks he has been ignored and goes on bidding.

Classes of move		Structure of move	Classes of act
Opening (pupil)	Sir. Sir. Can I go to the toilet?	sel sel h	bid bid elicitation
Answering	Yes.	h	reply
Opening (teacher to another child)	If you've got a printed one you shouldn't have.	h	comment
Opening (pupil)	Sir. Can I go to the toilet?	sel h	bid elicitation
Opening (pupil)	Sir. Please can I go to the toilet?	sel h	bid elicitation
Opening	Climb over that way	h	directive

(Text H)

Answering moves have a simpler structure; a maximum of three elements, pre-head, head, and post-head, and very often only the head occurs. There are three types of head appropriate to the three heads of opening moves. The response appropriate to an informative is simply acknowledgement that one is listening, and this can be, and usually is in the classroom, non-verbal. Following a directive the head of an answering move is realized by react, but the pupil may also acknowledge verbally that he

47

has heard. Following an elicitation there is a reply, and sometimes a comment as well.

Classes of move		Structure of move	Classes of act
Opening	Well, what leads you to believe he's like that?	s h	marker elicitation
Answering	He's rather free to—rather free in criticizing somebody else yet he might not like to be criticized himself. Criticizing the local councillor, it's not right really.	h post-h	reply comment

(Text F)

Follow-up, the third class of move in teaching exchanges is an
interesting category. Its function is to let the pupil know how
well he/she has performed. It is very significant that follow-up
occurs not only after a pupil answering move, but also after a
pupil opening move when the head is realized by an informative.
In other words the teacher often indicates the value of an
unelicited contribution from a pupil, usually in terms of relevance to the discourse.

Follow-up has a three-term structure, pre-head, head, post-
head, realized by accept, evaluate, and comment respectively.

Classes of move		Structure of move	Classes of act
Opening	Do you know what we mean by accent?	h	elicitation
Answering	It's the way you talk.	h	reply
Follow-up	The way we talk. This is a very broad comment.	pre-h h	accept evaluate

(Text F)

48

The act evaluate is seen by all participants as a compulsory element. A teacher can produce a follow-up move which overtly consists of only accept or comment, but evaluation is then implicit (and usually unfavourable). Very frequently, if the teacher only accepts a reply, the class offers another reply without any prompting.

The structure and classes of exchanges

There are two major classes of exchange, *Boundary* and *Teaching*. The function of boundary exchange is, as the name suggests, to signal the beginning or end of what the teacher considers to be a stage in the lesson; teaching exchanges are the individual steps by which the lesson progresses. Boundary exchanges consist of two moves, framing and focusing; often the two occur together, the framing move frequently occurs on its own, the focusing move does so only rarely. A typical boundary exchange is:

Class of move		Structure of move
Framing	Well ∧	marker, silent stress
Focusing	Today	metastatement

(Text D)

The definition of teaching exchange given above is vague, but there are eleven sub-categories with specific functions and unique structures. Of the eleven sub-categories six are *Free* exchanges and five are *Bound*. The function of bound exchanges is fixed because they either have no initiating move, or have an initiating move without a head, which simply serves to reiterate the head of the preceding free initiation.

Free exchanges

The six free exchanges are divided into four groups according to function, and two of the groups are further subdivided according to whether teacher or pupil initiates, because there are different structural possibilities. The four main functions of exchanges are informing, directing, eliciting, and checking, and they are distinguished by the type of act which realizes the head of the initiating move, informative, directive, elicitation, and check respectively. The structure of each of these exchanges will now be exemplified.

Each exchange type is given a number and a functional label, and the characteristic structure noted. The structure is expressed in terms of Initiation (I), Response (R), Feedback (F); moves are coded across the page with three main columns for Opening, Answering, and Follow-up, while the narrow columns give the move structure in terms of acts. A single line across the page signifies an exchange boundary, so one reads down the first column until one comes to the boundary line, then down the second column, and then down the third column. Each act begins on a separate line.

I Teacher Inform

This exchange is used when the teacher is passing on facts, opinions, ideas, new information to the pupil. Pupils may, but usually do not, make a verbal response to the teacher's initiation. Thus the structure is I (R); there is no feedback.

Opening		Answering	Follow-up
now, luckily, the French could read Greek.	m i		

(Text A)

II Teacher Direct

This category covers all exchanges designed to get the pupil to do but not say something. Because of the nature of the classroom, the Response is a compulsory element of structure. This is not to suggest that children always do what they are told, but it does imply that the teacher has a right to expect the pupil to do so. Just as anyone can produce an ungrammatical sentence when he feels like it, so a pupil can break the rules of discourse. Feedback is not an essential element of this structure although it frequently occurs. The structure is I R (F).

50

Opening		Answering		Follow-up
I want you to take your pen and I want you to rub it as hard as you can on something woollen.	d	Activity	rea	

(Text G)

III   Teacher Elicit

This category includes all exchanges designed to obtain verbal contributions from pupils. Very frequently a teacher will use a series of elicit exchanges to move the class step by step to a conclusion. Sometimes an elicit is used in isolation in the middle of a series of informs to check that the pupils have remembered a fact. The elicit exchanges which occur in the classroom have a different function from most occurring outside the classroom. Usually when we ask a question we don't know the answer; almost invariably the teacher does know the answer and children can get quite annoyed if he doesn't—after all that's his job. This fact enables us to explain why feedback is an essential element in an exchange inside the classroom. Having given their reply children want to know whether it was the right one. So important is feedback that if it does not occur we feel confident in saying that the teacher has deliberately withheld it for some strategic purpose. It is deviant to withhold feedback continually, and we have a tape of one lesson where a teacher, new to a class, and trying to suggest to them that there aren't always right answers, does withhold feedback and eventually reduces the children to silence—they cannot see the point of his questions. Thus the structure of elicits differs from that of directs in that F is a compulsory element.

Opening		Answering		Follow-up	
What's the name of this cutter? Hands up. NV[1] Janet.	el cu b n	Hacksaw	rep	The hacksaw. And I'll put that one there.	e z

[1]NV = non-verbal move.

(Text H)

IV Pupil Elicit

In many classrooms children rarely ask questions and when they do they are mainly of the order 'Do we put the date' or 'Can I go to the lavatory'. Usually the child has to catch the teacher's attention and get permission to speak. (See Sacks 1972 on the ways children get into ordinary conversation.) This permission may not be granted. The initial bid may be countered with a 'not now' or 'just a minute' and the exchange never get off the ground. The crucial difference between teacher and pupil elicits is that the pupil provides no feedback—an evaluation of a teacher reply would be cheeky. Thus the structure is IR.

Opening			Answering		Follow-up
Mrs. H. Yes. Are the numbers for le—for the letters?	b n el		Yes. They're—that's the order, one, two, three, four.	rep com	

(Text C)

V Pupil Inform

Occasionally pupils offer information which they think is relevant, or interesting—they usually receive an evaluation of its worth and often a comment as well. Thus the structure is I F not I (R) as for teacher informs.

Opening		Answering	Follow-up	
Miss P. There's some—there's a letter's missing from that up and down one I can't see one.	b i		Oh yes. You're right. It is. I can't remember what it is.	acc e com

(Text D)

This example has been simplified by the omission of a *repeat* bound exchange, which will be described below.

VI   Check

At some time in most lessons teachers feel the need to discover how well the children are getting on, whether they can follow what is going on, whether they can hear. To do this they use a checking move which could be regarded as a sub-category of elicit, except that feedback is not essential, because these are real questions to which the teacher does *not* know the answer. Any evaluation is an evaluation of an activity or state not the response. Thus the structure is IR(F). A broken line between exchanges signifies that the second is bound to the first.

Opening		Answering		Follow-up	
Finished Joan?	ch⟨n⟩	NV	rep	Good girl	e
And Miri?	n	yes	rep	Good	e
Finished?	ch	yes	rep		

(Text D)

Bound exchanges

Of the five types of bound exchange, four are bound to teacher elicits, and one to a teacher direct. As we said above, an exchange is bound either if it has no initiating move, or if the initiating move it does have has no head, but simply consists of nomination, prompt, or clue.

VII   Re-initiation (i)

When the teacher gets no reponse to an elicitation he can start again using the same or a rephrased question or he can use one or more of the acts—prompt, nomination, clue—to re-initiate. The original elicitation stands and these items are used as a second attempt to get a reply. This gives a structure of I R I^b R F, where I^b is a bound initiation.

Opening		Answering		Follow-up	
What is 'comprehend'?	el	Ø			
Nicola?	n	Ø			
In fact if you get this word, you'll comprehend. NV David again.	cl b n	Find out.	rep	Yes find out.	e

(Text A)

VIII Re-initiation (ii)

When a teacher gets a wrong answer there are two major routes open to him: he can stay with the same child and try by Socratic method to work him round to the right answer or he can keep the question and move on to another child. This type of re-initiation differs from the previous one in that feedback does occur. It is usually realized by 'Yes', 'No' or a repetition of what the pupil has just said, with a tone 3 intonation indicating incompleteness or a tone 4 intonation indicating reservation. An initiating move is not essential for the bound exchange, but if it does occur it is realized by prompt, nomination, or clue. This gives a structure of I R F (I^b) R F.

Opening		Answering		Follow-up	
This I think is a super one. Isobel. Can you think what it means?	s n el	Does it mean there's been an accident further down the road?	rep	No [3]	e
		Does it mean a double bend ahead?	rep	No [3]	e
Look at the car.	cl	Slippery roads?	rep	Yes. It means 'Be careful because the road's very slippery'.	e com

(Text D)

IX Listing

Occasionally teachers withhold evaluation until they get two or three answers. Sometimes they are making sure that more than one person knows the answer, sometimes they have asked a multiple question. In this case the structure is exactly the same as for Re-initiation (ii), I R F (I^b) R F (I^b) R F, but the realization of two of the elements is different. I^b is only realized by nomination and the F preceding I^b contains no evaluation.

Opening		Answering		Follow-up	
What's the name of each one of those?	el	Paper clip.	rep	Paper clip.	acc
		Nail.	rep	Nail.	acc
		Nut and bolt.	rep	Nut and bolt. [1+]	e

(Text H)

X Reinforce

Very occasionally in the tapes there is a bound exchange following a teacher direct. They occur when the teacher has told the class to do something and one child is slow or reluctant or hasn't fully understood. The structure is I R I^b R, with the I^b realized by a clue, prompt or nomination. In the following example a West Indian boy has misunderstood the directive.

Opening		Answering		Follow-up
I want you to take your pen and I want you to rub it as hard as you can on something woollen.	d	ACTIVITY	rea	
Not in your hair, on your jumper.	cl	ACTIVITY	rea	

(Text G)

XI Repeat

In every communicative situation there will be times when

someone does not hear. There are no examples in our tapes of a child admitting to not hearing but teachers do so quite frequently. Thus instead of feedback following the pupil response we get a bound initiation. Of course teachers can and do use this exchange when they have heard, but want a reply repeated for other reasons. The structure is I R I^b R F.

Opening		Answering		Follow-up	
What are you laughing at Rebecca?	el $\langle n \rangle$	Nothing	rep		
Pardon	loop	Nothing	rep	You're laughing at nothing	acc

(Text F)

The structure of transactions

Transactions normally begin with a Preliminary exchange and end with a Final exchange. Within these boundaries a series of medial exchanges occur. Although we have identified eleven types of medial exchanges we cannot yet specify in detail how they are ordered within transactions. We can specify that the first medial exchange in a transaction will normally be selected from the three major teacher-initiated free exchange types—*Inform*, *Direct*, and *Elicit*. Following a selection of one of these types, characteristic options occur in the rest of the transaction.

From now on what we say will be much more speculative and we will be talking about ideal types of transaction. We have not yet done enough work on transactions to be sure that what we suggest here will stand up to detailed investigation. We provisionally identify three major transaction types, informing, directing, and eliciting. Their basic structures will be outlined below. We do not, however, in an analysis of texts yet feel sufficiently confident in an identification of these structures to make the labelling of these transaction types a major element of coding.

Informing transactions

$$
T \begin{cases}
E & - & \text{Boundary} \\
E & - & \text{T–Inform} \\
(\langle E \rangle)^n & - & \text{T–Elicit} \\
(\langle E \rangle)^n & - & \text{P–Elicit} \\
E & - & \text{Boundary}
\end{cases}
$$

(The round brackets indicate that an item is optional, the diamond brackets that it occurs inside the previous item.)

During a lengthy informing exchange from the teacher, the pupils do little but acknowledge. However, embedded within an informing transaction may be brief teacher elicitations, used to keep attention or to check that pupils are understanding, and also pupil elicitations on some point raised by the teacher.

Directing transactions

$$
T \begin{cases}
E & - & \text{Boundary} \\
E & - & \text{T–Direct} \\
(E)^n & - & \text{P–Elicit} \\
(E)^n & - & \text{P–Inform} \\
E & - & \text{T–Elicit} \\
E & - & \text{Boundary}
\end{cases}
$$

This structure occurs where a T–Direct exchange stands at the head of a transaction, rather than in a subordinate position. The directive will usually be one requesting pupils to engage in some work on their own, for example working out some cartouches, or writing a sentence in hieroglyphs. When pupils are working separately, they have most opportunity for initiating exchanges. They can make comments on, or ask questions about their task, and ask for evaluation of their work. Characteristically the teacher ends such a transaction with an elicitation asking for the pupils' answers or results.

Eliciting transactions

$$
T \begin{cases}
E & - & \text{Boundary} \\
E^n & - & \text{T–Elicit} \\
E & - & \text{Boundary}
\end{cases}
$$

When the teacher is asking questions, the pupils contribute

P–Elicit	Sir how did this man manage to work out the names of the people?	el	Because he was clever, that's how.	rep

(Text A)

T–Elicit	What did they call their leaders, their rulers?	el	Emperors	rep	No, not emperors	e
Re–Initiate			Pharaohs	rep	Pharaohs, yes. And that's what that one is and they used to worship them.	e com
P–Elicit	What were Popes?	el	Still have Popes. The Pope's the Head of the Catholic Church	rep	mm Oh.	acc acc
T–Elicit	Where does he live?	el	Rome.	rep	Rome yes.	e
T-Elicit	Do you know which part of Rome?	el				
	He's got a separate little country in Rome a separate little country	cl				

(Text C)

continually to the discourse by making verbal responses, but they have little opportunity to initiate exchanges. When a pupil does break out of the usual structure with an elicitation, and this is rare, it does not lead to a series of pupil elicitations. The teacher quickly resumes the initiating role either by refusing an adequate answer as in Text A, or by taking over the pupil's topic as in Text C.

We have so far mentioned only the characteristic places in the structure of transactions at which three teacher-initiated, and two pupil-initiated exchanges can occur. Even more tentatively we can suggest that the teacher-initiated check exchange typically occurs in a directing transaction before the final elicit exchange. The teacher here is usually checking on pupils' progress with the task he directed them to do at the beginning of the transaction.

We can specify no ordering for the bound exchanges. They occur after a T–Direct or T–Elicit exchange, but whether any or all occur, and in what order, is dependent on unpredictable reactions to and involvement with the teacher's presentation of the topic.

The structure of lessons

The lesson is the highest unit of classroom discourse, made up of a series of transactions. If the pupils are responsive and co-operative, the discourse unit 'lesson' may approximate closely to any plan the teacher may have formulated for presenting his chosen topic. He may have decided, for example, to start off by presenting some information, to continue by discovering whether the information has been assimilated, and then to get the pupils to use the information he has presented in their own work. Alternatively a teacher might begin with a series of elicit exchanges, attempting to move the pupils towards conclusions which will later be elaborated in an informing transaction. However, a variety of things can interfere in the working-out of the teacher's plan in actual discourse. The structure of the lesson is affected by such performance features as the teacher's own memory capacity for ordering speech, and, more importantly, the need to respond to unpredicted reactions, misunderstandings or contributions on the part of the pupils.

We cannot specify any ordering of transactions into lessons. To do this would require a much larger sample of classroom discourse. We might find, for example, that there are characteristic lesson structures for different subjects, or for different teachers. At the moment, however, we must think of the 'lesson' as a stylistic type, which means that strictly there is little point in labelling the lesson as a unit. We could describe the ordering of transactions into lessons in the texts we have, but that ordering varies for each teacher and we can identify no restrictions on the occurrence of different types.

4 ANALYSED TEXTS

This chapter consists of two analysed texts—the first is a complete lesson from our original set of controlled recordings; the second was sent to us when we began to collect uncontrolled data and is not a complete lesson. The teacher is using the matrix unit materials from *Concept 7–9* with a class of eight- to nine-year-olds in a school with 72% West Indian and Asian immigrant children.

Our aim in presenting these analysed texts is twofold. Firstly, we want to give readers a clear idea of how the data was handled. Where research follows a well-established methodology this is unnecessary; however, when one is in the preliminary stages of devising a methodological approach to data, a lengthy exemplification is essential. Secondly, we are anxious that others should be able to use our descriptive method, and for them a large amount of analysed text is an essential test for their understanding of the method.

CONVENTIONS USED IN TRANSCRIPTION AND ANALYSIS

The layout of texts follows the conventions developed in Chapter 3. The major points are:

(a) Transaction boundaries are marked by a double line, exchange boundaries by a single line. When one exchange is bound to a preceding exchange this is indicated by a broken line.

(b) The page is divided into three columns for opening, answering, and follow-up moves. One reads down the first column until one reaches a horizontal line across the page, then reads down the second column to the line, then down the third column.

(c) Ideally the page would be divided into five columns to allow for framing and focusing moves, but restrictions on space have caused us to put these moves in the opening column. We indicate that they are not opening moves by removing the columns for answering and follow-up moves.

(d) An additional column has been added to the left-hand side to enable us to label the exchange type, which in Chapter 3 occurred above the piece of analysis.

(e) In general, exchanges are initiated by teachers; when a pupil does make an opening move this is shown by prefixing the exchange label with P. Thus a pupil-initiated eliciting exchange would be labelled P-Elicit.

(f) Where necessary in follow-up moves we indicate intonation by placing the reference number of the tone group in square brackets. Thus a low rising tone which signals something more is required is indicated by [3], a rising tone which questions a pupil answer by [2], a rising falling rising tone which implies reservation by [4], a high falling tone which shows strong agreement by [1+] and a low falling tone which accepts but does not evaluate the response by [1−].

(g) If an act is cancelled paralinguistically by the teacher immediately it has been uttered this is symbolized by a diagonal line, e͠l.

(h) Non-verbal surrogates of discourse acts are represented by NV.

(i) Diamond brackets are used to show that one element of structure is included within another. Thus 'I wonder what Andrew thinks about this one?' is el⟨n⟩.

TEXT D

Exchange Type	Opening	Act	Answering	Act	Follow-up	Act
Boundary	Well ∧ FRAME	m				
	Today I thought we'd do three quizzes. We won't take the whole lesson to do a quiz because I want to talk to you some of the time. FOCUS	ms				
		com				
Direct	The first quiz is this.	s				
	Can you fill in this sentence.	s				
	See if you can do it in your books.	d	NV	rea		
Check	Finished Joan?	ch⟨n⟩	NV	rep	Good girl.	
Re-Initiate	And Miri?	n	Yes.	rep	Good.	
Check	Finished?	ch	Yes.	rep		
Boundary	Right ∧ FRAME	m				
Elicit	Read us what you've written, Joan.	el	The cat sat on the rug.	rep	Yes that's right. I changed the last word.	e com

Exchange Type	Opening	Act	Answering	Act	Follow-up	Act
Elicit	Now / What are the letters that are missing?	m / el	e	rep	Yes. [3]	acc
Listing			a	rep	a [3]	acc
Listing			a	rep	Yes. [3]	acc
Listing			o	rep		
Re-Initiate	and?	p	e	rep		
Re-Initiate	and?	p	u	rep	u, Yes. [1]	e
Elicit	Those letters have special names. / Do you know what it is?	s / el	∅			
Elicit	What is one name we give to those letters? Paul.	el / n	er, vowels.	rep	They're vowels, aren't they.	e
Elicit	Do you think you could say that sentence without having the vowels in it?	el	∅			

	Teacher		NV	rep	Response	
Elicit	You knew what the vowels were because you'd heard, 'the cat sat on the mat'. I tricked, I cheated by changing the last word. Could you say it without the vowel sounds?	s s el	NV	rep	It's jolly hard isn't it. Ever so hard.	com
Elicit	Can you think why I changed 'mat' to 'rug'?	el	Because, er	rep		
Re-Initiate	Peter.	n	Mat's got two vowels in it	rep		
Elicit	Which are they? What are they?	el el	'a' and 't' 'a' and 't'	rep		
Elicit	Is 't' a vowel?	el	No.	rep	No. [1]	e
Elicit	Why did I put 'rug' instead of 'mat'?	el	Because nearly every sentence you see like that it's 'mat'.	rep	Yes. [1—]	acc
Elicit	But why did I change mine to rug?	el	'cos there's too many 'a's.	rep	He's near, isn't he. He's not quite there.	e
Re-Initiate			You wanted all the vowels in—	rep	I wanted all the vowels. I'd only got 'a', 'e', 'i'—	e com

Exchange Type	Opening	Act	Answering	Act	Follow-up	Act
Elicit	We haven't got them all in have we. What haven't we got?	s el	'i'	rep	'i' But we have got 'u'.	e com
Boundary	Right∧ FRAME	m				
	So that's the first quiz FOCUS and I think you got that all right.	con com				
Boundary	Right∧ FRAME	m				
	Here's the next quiz then if you're ready. FOCUS	ms				
Elicit	I want you to look at these	s	The first one's workmen.	rep		
	I don't want you to write anything.	s				
	But I just want you to look at them and see if you can tell me what these mean?	s el				
	NV	b				
	Ann.	n				
Repeat	This one?	l	NV	rep	Yes. [1—]	acc

Act	Code	Teacher	rep	Response	acc	Feedback
Elicit	el	Where would you see these signs?	rep	Where the men were digging the road up and making an open hole.		Yes. [1—]
Inform	i	It's a warning sign isn't it. It's a warning sign, so be careful because further along up the road that you're driving on there are some workmen digging up the road or filling in a hole, doing some work.				
Elicit	el cl n	What's the next one mean? You don't often see that one around here. Miri.	rep	Danger falling rocks.	e com	Danger, falling rocks. You're driving along—
Elicit	el b n	Where would you be driving d'you think if you— NV Yes.	rep	Round about Scotland in the mountain parts.	e com	In the mountains. I've seen these in Wales, but I haven't driven in Scotland recently.
Elicit	s s el⟨n⟩	What about this one. This, I think, is a super one. Isabel, can you think what it means?	rep	Does it mean there's been an accident further along the road?	e	No. [3]

Exchange Type	Opening	Act	Answering	Act	Follow-up	Act
Re-Initiate			Does it mean a double bend ahead?	rep	No. [3]	e
Re-Initiate	Look at the car.	cl	Er slippery roads?	rep	Yes. [1] It means 'be careful' because the road's very slippery.	e com
Elicit	What makes a road slippery?	el	You might have rain or snow on it.	rep	Yes, snow, ice.	e
Elicit	Anything else make a road slippery?	el	Erm oil?	rep	Oil makes it very slippery when it's mixed with water, doesn't it? The oil skims on top of the water.	e com
Boundary	Yes good. FRAME So those are all caution signs. FOCUS	m con				
Elicit	—but did you notice the difference between the first quiz you did and the second quiz?	el	One was words and one was	rep	One was words. [4]	e

Re-Initiate	and one was just—	p	Signs.	rep	Signs. [1 —]	acc
Re-Initiate	or—	p	Meanings.	rep	They have meanings. Yes. [1 —]	acc
Re-Initiate			Warnings.	rep	They are all warnings.	acc
Re-Initiate	I was thinking of a much simpler word than that.	cl	Pictures.	rep	Pictures! [1+] They're all pictures aren't they? They're all pictures then that could give us some warning. Erm, as Paul said, they're er they're—they're all symbols, er, drawn in pictures, with no words at all.	e / com
Elicit	This is a great advantage for motorists. Can you think why?	s el	Erm, cos as the motorist's driving along he doesn't have to read them as he's driving.	rep	He doesn't have to keep his eyes in two places all at once. He can just drive along and look, look at the pictures and think Ah hah! Yes be careful along	e

Exchange Type	Opening	Act	Answering	Act	Follow-up	Act
Boundary	So symbols really are extremely useful for us aren't they.	con				
Inform	Well this is, has been so for thousands and thousands of years. Because as long ago as three thousand years before Jesus Christ was born—	m i			here there's rocks falling on the road. I've got to drive very cautiously. Or, along here there are some workmen and I've got to make sure that I don't go down a hole or run them over, and he doesn't have to spend time reading words.	com
Elicit	—How long ago was that?	el	Five thousand years	rep	About five thousand years.	e

Move						
Inform	i	—Erm, a group of people used symbols to do their writing. They used pictures instead of, as we write, in words.				
Elicit	el p n	Do you know who those people were? I'm sure you do. Joan.	rep	The Egyptians.	e	The Egyptians.
Inform	z i	And—when I can find my chart—here it is. Here are some of the symbols that they used.				
Elicit	el	Can you say anything about those symbols?	rep	They're all easy to draw.	acc e com	Er yes. Reasonably easy to draw. That's a good point isn't it. Because if they were very complicated it wouldn't be very easy to put them on whatever you wanted to put them on.
Elicit	s el	Can you think of anything that they would be put on. Would they just be written or painted or drawn on the sand?	rep	They might be on the rocks.	e	Yes they were mainly carved in rocks.

Exchange Type	Opening	Act	Answering	Act	Follow-up	Act
Elicit	And these symbols have a special name. Does anybody know that special name?	s el	Is it Arabic?	rep	No, it isn't Arabic.	e
Inform	Well, they're called hiero-glyphics. Hieroglyphics. It's hieroglyphic writing. And these, each one of these is an hieroglyph.	i				
Inform	Can you see that each one stands for a particular sound. This one for the our letter 't' which make would make the sound 't', wouldn't it. Erm this one a 'ch' sound.	i				
Elicit	Have a quick look and see if you can see anything that you think is rather peculiar?	el	There's two haitches	rep	Yes some of them are duplicated, aren't they. There are two symbols for one sound. I haven't yet been able to find out why this is. I've got	e com

		FRAME			
Boundary	Well ∧	m			
Inform	these symbols, these hiero-glyphs were carved into the rocks of the tombs of the great kings of Egypt. And usually, erm, the king would have his name carved in the er his tomb. And these here are the names of some great people who lived at that particular time.	i			
Elicit	Of course you can guess what the third quiz is going to be, can't you. What's it going to be?	s / el	Find out what the name of the—	s / rep / e	Yes. Finding out what the names, the names that appear on the— / some books that we can look at just now to see if we can find out just why it is.
Inform	—This is called a cartouche by the way. This special shape and I believe it's a word that means bullet-shaped bullet-shaped.	i			

Exchange Type	Opening	Act	Answering	Act	Follow-up	Act
Boundary	So that that's the next FOCUS quiz, and we'll do that just now.	s ms				
Elicit	Now I wonder how you are able or we are able to say, 'Well, erm, that is the symbol, the sign for the sound 'p'.' I wonder how we are able to do this.	s el	φ			
Inform	And people weren't able to do this until, about a hundred and seventy years ago. When some French soldiers dug up, found a stone that was called that is called the Rosetta Stone, which was once in the tomb of a very great king of Egypt, and on it was carved signs like this, symbols, but also two other languages. This was the middle line. The top one was carved in—the top row of writing was in Greek. The next row was in hieroglyphs like this and the next one was	i				

	a shorthand of this version of writing. You can imagine how long it would take if you'd got to write, draw a picture for each letter, and so the Egyptians evolved a short-hand way of writing these. When the stone was dug up—er until that time, people were still in the dark about hiero-glyph erm symbols. But as the first row was in Greek, scholars, clever people, were able to translate it.					
Elicit	And then they realized that what was on the second row was really repetition of what was on the—	el	first	rep	First row.	e
Elicit	and what was on the third row was really a repetition again of what appeared on the—	el	first	rep	First and second rows.	e
Inform	And so they were able to translate and this is what they this is the result of the work that they did. They found that these were the symbols which meant these sounds.	i				

Exchange Type	Opening	Act	Answering	Act	Follow-up	Act
Direct	These three then are for you to sort out for yourselves.	s				
	Can you translate can you be an Egyptologist and translate these names from this chart.	d				
	I'll put them along here so that you can see them.	z				
Inform	Now	m				
	They won't they're not easy words and they're not words that are spelled exactly as we'd spell them in our own language. They're spelled actually in Greek. One of them is such a funny word. One is a famous Queen. One is a warrior. And the funniest one of all is the great king who had the Rosetta Stone made and put in his tomb.					
Direct	Now you can do them in any order you like.	s				
	Let us see if you can sort out which is which.	d	NV	rea		

Move	Text		Yes	rep	All right then	acc
Elicit	Shall we do them all together?	el				
Elicit	Let's do this one here first shall we. Can you see a creature that looks like this?—	s el				
Inform	—Oh, another thing that I must tell you, and that is the fact that, er, sometimes the Egyptians didn't bother to put in all the vowel sounds.	i				
Check	Do you remember our 'The cat sat on the rug'?	ch	mm	rep	Sometimes those might be missing.	com
Inform	This is a reason why we're not quite sure whether our pronunciation of Egyp old Egyptian words is quite right because, let's face it, if you wrote your name with two or three of the letters missing, you're not going to be able to your friends aren't going to be able to say it properly, are they.	i				
Boundary	All right then ∧	FRAME m				

Exchange Type	Opening	Act	Answering	Act	Follow-up	Act
Elicit	I think all of them are in this one. So let's see what's the first one.	s el	Ø			
Elicit	Can you see one that looks like that? NV Yes.	el b n	'a' and 'h'	rep	Right.	e
Direct	Write these down to translate them.	d	NV	rea		
Elicit	What's number two?	el	'l'	rep	The sound 'l'. The letter 'l'. Yes.	e
Elicit	The next one?	el	't'	rep		
Re-Initiate	Janet.	n	'k'	rep	'k', yes.	e
Elicit	The next one?	el	's'	rep	Yes.	e
Elicit	Can you say that so far?	el	'ahlks'	rep		
Elicit	Is it how we'd spell it normally?	el	No.	rep		

Direct	Finish it off then quickly. Let's see who's going to be first.	d			rea	
P-Inform	NV Yes. Miss, there's some, there's a letter's missing for that up and down one I can't see one.	b n i				
Repeat	This one?	l	Number six, Miss.	rep	Oh yes. You're right. It is.	acc e
Direct	Miss it out.	d				
Direct	Leave a space for it.	d				
Inform	I can't remember what it is.	i				
Check	Have you got it?	ch	Yes.	rep		
Elicit	What's the name?	el	I can't say it.	rep		
Elicit	Who'll who'll try and say it?	el	Ø			
Re-Initiate	Well you've said the first part.	cl	Alek Aleks	rep	I hope I've got it right.	com
Re-Initiate	NV Yes.	b n	Does it say aliksia? aloksaidros?	rep	No, not quite.	e

Exchange Type	Opening	Act	Answering	Act	Follow-up	Act
Elicit	Well try the next word, let's see if you can get that one. What's the first letter?	s el	'k'. 'k' or 'q'	rep		
Direct	Try it then.	d	NV	rea		
Inform	It's 'n' this squiggly one 'N'	i	mm	ack		
Direct	Put down an 'n'. Or the sound for 'n'	d z	NV	rea		
Elicit	Can anyone have a guess, a shot at that one?	el	Cleopatra.	rep	Cleopatra. Good girl. She was the most famous queen, wasn't she, Cleopatra of the Nile.	e com
Boundary	Right ∧ FRAME	m				
Direct	Try the last one.	d	NV	rea		
Re-Initiate	Come on, Isabel. You're nearly there.	p⟨n⟩ cl	Ø			
Re-Initiate	It begins with 'pt'	cl	Ptolmees.	rep	Yes, Ptolemy. That's his name. Yes. Isn't it a funny name.	e com

Inform	Well that was the great king who ordered his, er, men, his servant, his slaves to carve out in the rock, er, the three sets of writing. He wanted to show people who possible would—although I don't think he wanted people to see inside his tomb—but he wanted people that lived after him to see the three different kinds of writing that were in use when he was king.	i				
Elicit	Who knows anything about these. What do we call them? Er, kings of Egypt. We don't call them kings really. They have a special name.	s el cl	Pharaohs.	rep	They were Pharaohs.	e
Elicit	Erm, do you know anything that they did, anything about them?	el	ϕ			
Re-Initiate	Well, they were great ones for building something that you make in Maths, weren't they, to start with?	cl	Pyramids.	rep	Pyramids. Yes.	e

Exchange Type	Opening	Act	Answering	Act	Follow-up	Act
Elicit	What are Pyramids?	el	Ø			
Elicit	Why did they build Pyramids? Paul.	el n	When they were dead they put all their riches and everything they owned in their Pyramid.	rep	Yes they did, yes. Right in the depth, in the heart of the Pyramid there was a special little room where they had their personal belongings. Precious special things that belonged to them.	e com
Elicit	Can you suggest the sort of things that might be with them? NV Yes.	el b n	Jewels.	rep	Their own special jewels. [3] The ones that they liked the best. [3]	e com
Re-Initiate			Their robes.	rep	Clothes. [3] Yes. [1 –]	e acc
Re-Initiate			The couch they liked best.	rep	Yes, their favourite chair or throne or couch. [3]	e

Move	Utterance	Act	Utterance	Act	Utterance	Act
Re-Initiate			Their statue.	rep	Yes [3] Lots of statues have been found. [3] Yes. [1] So that erm that's how we know how they looked.	e / com
Elicit	Erm, they also had things like, er, model boats and chariots and, erm, bows and arrows and weapons. Why do you think they had these things put in their tombs? NV Paul the only one? NV Peter.	s / el / b / cu / b / n	To guard against evil.	rep	That's a good idea. I'm sure that that possibly crossed their minds.	e / com
Re-Initiate	That wasn't the only reason though.	cl	Because they thought when they died they go to, er, not to heaven, a place where they would then live again.	rep	Yes. They, they firmly believed—this was the whole point of doing it—that they were going to live in another place, they were just going to move on into another life. And	e / com

Exchange Type	Opening	Act	Answering	Act	Follow-up	Act
Boundary	So that then is why the Pharaohs built their Pyramids—which really were great tombs—in which they were placed. FOCUS	con			so from this life he would want to take with him all the things that had given him pleasure and all the things that he would need to use. So he would take his boat in case he had to cross water. He would take his chariot if he wanted to drive along the road. And his favourite throne, and his favourite couch.	com
Elicit	And the Egyptians also had a very special art of doing something to people's bodies when they had died. What was this called?	s / el	They used to take out their heart and their brain, and put them in—	rep	They certainly did something special with their heart. [4] Yes. [5]	e

Move	Act	Initiation	Act	Response	Act	Feedback
Re-Initiate			rep	They wrapped the Pharaoh or the person up with a pile of bandages and put them in a kind of case. They were called mummies.	e	Yes. [1]
Elicit	el	What is the word then for doing putting this body in its mummy case? What did they—	rep	Mummify.	e / com	—They mummified it that means—yes. They drained out all the liquid from the body and rubbed special preserving oils into the body, wrapped it in bandages and put it in the case.
P-Inform	b / n / i	NV Yes. Miss, they showed you a Pharaoh's body mummified on 'Blue Peter'.			acc	Did they.
Elicit	el	When was this?	rep	On Monday I think.	acc	Good gracious me, that's fairly recently.

Exchange Type	Opening	Act	Answering	Act	Follow-up	Act
Elicit	Do you remember which one it was?	el	No Miss.	rep	No. [3]	acc
Re-Initiate	What about you Paul?	n	No Miss.	rep	No. [1 –]	acc
Elicit	Was it one that they were they photographs of erm a mummy case that they'd taken in a museum or—	el	Miss they had it there.	rep		
Repeat	Actually in the studio?	l	Yes.	rep	Gosh. That was exciting then, wasn't it.	acc
P-Inform	Miss they showed you a film about them moving the Egyptian temples to somewhere else.	i			Ah yes.	acc
Elicit	Why have they done this this great enormous temples. Had to be taken in great huge, enormous, gargantuan pieces and moved to other parts of Egypt.	el cl	Because some people are making a vast dam and they want to build on that place that it was before.	rep	Yes. [1 –]	acc

Elicit	What are they going to build?	el	They are going to build a big dam.	rep	Yes. [1+] They're going—the Valley of Kings was going to be flooded with water, wasn't it. Because they want the water for irrigation.	e com
Elicit	And also, I think, for . . .	el	The people?	rep	Yes. [1−]	acc
Elicit	Aren't they going to build a hydro-electric dam there?	el	Yes.	rep		
Inform	A hydro-electric dam to produce electricity for the people of Egypt. Er, an enormous project which has been going on for a few years now, and, er, great pieces of rock have been hewn out of these temples which are, which were actually made in the rock face itself. These have been all cut out, and each one has been carefully numbered so when it's carted off and taken away somewhere else it can all be fitted together again, er, to make it complete, so that people can see it.	i				

Exchange Type	Opening	Act	Answering	Act	Follow-up	Act
P-Inform	Miss the er London Bridge they're transporting that to America.	i			Yes, they are aren't they. They're building that somewhere else.	e com
Elicit	Have a word about this chap we don't seem to have finished do we?	el	ø			
Elicit	What's the first the first little bit makes sense, say the first syllable. You say it to me. Come on.	el n p	Alec.	rep	Alex, doesn't it say Alex.	e
Elicit	Well, do you know a man's name— Can you finish that off?	s el	Alexander.	rep	Alexander. I think it's Alexander the Great.	e com
Inform	Do you know anything about him? I don't know much about him only that he was a great warrior king though a great leader. That's something else for you to find out about.	s i				

Boundary	Well ∧ FRAME to finish with then. FOCUS	m ms				
Direct	I've got these two books that Miss MacDonald found for me, and I thought you'd like to look through these at your leisure and see what you can find out about the hieroglyphics perhaps you may like to find out about mummies and tombs.	s d				
Boundary	So there you are then you can have five minutes with those.	ms				
Elicit	Who got all the three names right by the way?	el	Φ			
Elicit	Who got two and a half right who got the . . .	el	NV	rep	Yes.	acc
Elicit	Who got the Ptolemy one right? I never know whether to say Ptolemy or Tommy or Thomy.	el com	I did.	rep	You did? Good well done.	acc e
Boundary	Splendid ∧ FRAME	m				

89

TEXT H

Exchange Type	Opening	Act	Answering	Act	Follow-up	Act
Boundary	Now ʌ FRAME	m				
Direct	All eyes on me.	d	NV	rea		
Direct	Put your pencils down.	d	NV	rea		
Direct	Fold your arms.	d	NV	rea		
Direct	Hands on your heads.	d	NV	rea		
Direct	Hands on your shoulders.	d	NV	rea		
Direct	Fold your arms.	d	NV	rea		
Direct	Look at me.	d	NV	rea		
Elicit	Hands up. / What's that?	cu / el	Paper clip.	rep	A paper clip good. / A paper clip. [1–] / There we are.	e / acc / z
Elicit	And what's that? / Janet.	el / n	A nail.	rep	A nail well done. / A nail. [1–]	e / acc
Elicit	And hands up. / What's that one? / That's got two names a double name.	cu / el / cl	A nut and bolt.	rep	A nut and bolt good boy a nut and bolt.	e

		s				e
Elicit	And what do we call this thing? What's this a bit of? NV Yes.	el b n	A piece of metal.	rep	A piece of metal good boy.	e
Direct	Can you point to a piece of metal in this room anybody a piece of metal in this room.	d	NV	rea	Yes.	e
Direct	*You* go and show me one David a piece of metal.	d⟨n⟩	NV	rea	Yes that's a piece of metal well done a team point you can have one.	e
Direct	Will *you* show me a piece of metal.	d⟨n⟩	NV	rea	Yes the radiator that's a piece of metal.	e
Elicit	Hands up. What's that what's that? NV Yes Cleveland.	cu el b n	Piece of wood.	rep	Piece of wood good piece of wood.	e
Direct	Point to a piece of wood everyone, piece of wood anywhere.	d n	NV	rea	Yes that's fine.	e

Exchange Type	Opening	Act	Answering	Act	Follow-up	Act
Elicit	And hands up. What's that what's that? NV Janet.	cu el b n	Paper.	rep	Piece of paper.	e
Direct	Point to a piece of paper. Touch a piece of paper touch a piece of paper near you.	s d	NV	rea	Good, that's fine too. Piece of paper.	e com
Elicit	And can you tell me now what this is? Stephen Chapman.	el n	Pair of scissors.	rep	Pair of scissors.	e
Repeat	What is it?	l	Pair of scissors. CHORUS	rep	Pair of scissors. Yes pair of scissors.	e
Elicit	And this. What's this a picture of? Abdul.	s el n	Hacksaw.	rep	A hacksaw yes a hacksaw.	e
Boundary	Fine ^ FRAME	m				
Elicit	And the last picture of all, I've got there what's that? Danny.	el n	An axe.	rep	An axe yes it's an axe.	e

Boundary	Now then ∧ FRAME	m		rep		e
Elicit	I've got some things here, too. Hands up. What's that what is it?	s cu el	Saw.	rep	It's a saw yes this is a saw.	e
Elicit	What do we do with a saw?	el	Cut wood.	rep	Yes. You're shouting out though.	e com
Elicit	What do we do with a saw? Marvelette.	el n	Cut wood.	rep	We cut wood.	e
Elicit	And, erm, what do we do with— Well first of all what is this what is it?	el m el	Hacksaw.	rep	It's a hacksaw.	e
Elicit	What do we do with a hack-saw this hacksaw?	el	Cut trees.	rep		
Elicit	Do we cut trees with this?	el	No No.	rep		
Elicit	Hands up. What do we do with this?	cu el	Cut wood (INDISTINCT)	rep		
Elicit	Do we cut wood with this?	el	No.	rep		

Exchange Type	Opening	Act	Answering	Act	Follow-up	Act
Elicit	What do we do with that then?	el	Cut wood.	rep	We cut wood with that.	e
Elicit	What do we do with that? Sir. Cleveland.	el b n	Metal.	rep	We cut metal yes we cut metal.	e
Elicit	And, er, I've got this here. What's that? Trevor.	s el n	An axe.	rep	It's an axe yes.	e
Elicit	What do I cut with the axe?	el	Wood wood.	rep	Yes I cut wood with the axe.	e
Boundary	Right ∧ FRAME	m				
Inform	Now then I've got some more things here that cut things that you've seen before I think.	m i				
Elicit	Scissors What do I cut with scissors?	s el	Paper paper.	rep	Yes paper.	e
Direct	Somebody's shouting out at the back.	d	NV	rea		

Elicit	s el	And I've got some more cutters here. What's that cutter called?	A knife.	rep	A knife yes.	e
Elicit	el	What do I cut with a knife?	Food.	rep	I cut food.	e
Elicit	el	What kind of food would you cut with a knife?	Meat.	rep		
Listing	n	*You* tell me.	Fish.	rep	Fish. Yes. [3]	e
Listing			Meat.	rep	Meat. Yes. [3]	e
Elicit	el	What else would you cut with a knife?	Sausages.	rep	Sausages. Yes. [3]	e
Listing			Chicken.	rep	Chicken fine that's lovely.	e
Elicit	m s el	Now I've got a cutter here that you may not have seen before, a different cutter. Not scissors, but a cutter like that.	Pliers.	rep	No, not pliers.	e
P-Inform	i	It's like a pliers.			Like a pliers yes.	e
Elicit	el	What do you think this cuts?	It's like—cuts cuts metal things.	rep	It cuts metal things good boy yes.	e

Exchange Type	Opening	Act	Answering	Act	Follow-up	Act
Boundary	Let's have a look at these things lets have a look at these.　FOCUS (PAUSE 6 SECONDS)	ms				
Boundary	Now∧　FRAME Let's just have a look at these things here.　FOCUS	m ms				
Elicit	Can you tell me, first of all, what's this?	el	Paper.	rep	Piece of paper yes.	e
Elicit	And, hands up. What cutter will cut this?	cu	The pair of scissors.	rep	The pair of scissors yes.	e
Inform	Here we are, the pair of scissors. And, as you can see, it's going to cut the paper.	s i				
Elicit	Tell me what's this?	el	Cigarette box.	rep	Yes. [1⌐]	acc
Elicit	What's it made from?	el	Cardboard.	rep	Cardboard yes. [1]	e

Elicit	What will cut the cardboard?	el	Scissors. / Scissors.	rep / rep	Scissors yes.	e
Inform	Here we are then. / The scissors is cutting the / cardboard.	s / i				
Elicit	Now then, / what's this?	m / el	Piece of wool.	rep		
Repeat	Piece of—	l	Wool.	rep	Wool yes.	e
Elicit	What will cut the wool?	el	Scissors.	rep	The scissors yes.	e
Inform	There we are look. / There's the wool being cut by / the scissors.	s / i				
Elicit	Now / I've got a piece of what?	m / el	Wood.	rep	∅	
Elicit	What cuts the piece of wood? / Will the scissors cut the / piece of wood?	el / el	No.	rep	Let's try. / No it won't.	z / e
Elicit	Why won't the scissors cut / the piece of wood?	el	They weren't sharp / enough.	rep	Not sharp enough.	acc

Exchange Type	Opening	Act	Answering	Act	Follow-up	Act
Re-Initiate			The wood, the wood is hard.	rep	Because the wood is hard.	e
Elicit	What kind of things do the scissors cut?	el	Soft things.	rep	Soft things.	e
					Things like paper, and card and bits of wool like that but they won't cut the piece of wood.	com
Elicit	Let's see what we can use for the piece of wood.	s	Saw.	rep	The chopper yes.	e
	What cutter could we use for the piece of wood d'you think?	el	Chopper.	rep		
Elicit	What did we call it though?	el	Axe.	rep	We called it an axe yes we called it an axe.	e
Inform	And if I put it on here and I (CHOPS WOOD) do that it's cut in two pieces like that, there we are two pieces like that.	i				

		el		rep		e
Elicit	What else will cut the piece of wood?	el	Saw.	rep	The saw yes.	e
Inform	There's the saw. And I'll take a little bit of wood and put it on the edge of the desk and cut a bit off like that. (SAWS WOOD)	s / i				
P-Inform	Hacksaw isn't used for wood. (WHISPERED)	i	Isn't it?	ack		
Inform	There it is. It's cut through like that.	i				
Check	Can you see?	ch	Yes sir.	rep		
Inform	Piece of wood cut through with the saw.	con				
Boundary	Now then ∧ FRAME	m				
Elicit	Will this saw cut through this?	eˀ	No.	rep	It's metal yes.	e
	What is this?	el	Yeah. Metal.	rep rep		
Elicit	Will this saw cut through the metal?	el	No. Yes.	rep rep	It won't you know.	e

Exchange Type	Opening	Act	Answering	Act	Follow-up	Act
Elicit	Why won't it?	el	Because it's too hard.	rep	It's too hard yes. It's too hard for a wood saw.	e com
Elicit	What kind of a cutter have I got to use for this?	el	Hacksaw. Hacksaw.	rep rep	Hacksaw yes.	e
Inform	Here's my hacksaw. And I'm going to put it on here (SAWS METAL). Let me just put it over this piece of wood to protect the the desk.	s i z				
Elicit	And there it is. Can you see a piece of it's cut, like that and that?	s el				
Direct	Sit down Sta-er Stephen.	d	NV	rea		
Inform	There's a piece of metal cut.	i				
Elicit	And now I've got this thing. What metal is—what material is this?	s el	Iron.	rep		

				rep		e
Repeat	What is it? NV Yes.	l b n	Steel.	rep	No.	e
Elicit	It's not steel it's—	el	Metal. Iron.	rep rep	It is metal yes.	e
Elicit	Another name for it.	el	Tin. Iron.	rep rep	Tin yes. It's metal and it's tin.	e com
Boundary	And I'm going to see if this hacksaw will cut through. Here we go then. (SAWS TIN) FOCUS	ms				
Boundary	Now ∧ FRAME	m				
Check	Can you see where it's cut through the rough edge of the metal?	ch	Yes.	rep		
Boundary	Now now I'm going to take these things. FOCUS	ms				
Elicit	Now you couldn't tell me the name of these could you? What do you think they are?	m s el	Clippers.	rep	They are cutters.	e

Exchange Type	Opening	Act	Answering	Act	Follow-up	Act
Elicit	What do you think they will cut? They look to be very big and heavy and quite sharp.	el cl	Metal	rep	Yes they're metal cutters.	e
Inform	Just look. I take metal. (CUTS METAL) And can you see how it's cut through.	s s i	Wow! Cor!	ack ack		
Inform	—Those are very very sharp indeed.	i				
Elicit	Would you use these for cutting things like paper and cardboard?	el	No. CHORUS	rep	No.	e
Elicit	What would you use for those?	el	Scissors.	rep	Yes. You would use scissors for those soft things.	e acc
Elicit	Would you use this for cutting bread?	el	No.	rep		

Move	Text	act		Text	act	Text	act
Elicit	Hands up. What would you use for cutting bread?	cu / el		Knife. Knife.	rep / rep	A knife yes.	e
Direct	You're shouting out though and I don't want you to shout out.	d					
Elicit	What would you use for cutting wood?	el		Saw.	rep	A saw, good boy.	e
Elicit	What would you use if you were going to sharpen a pencil? If you were going to cut a pencil?	el / el		Knife.	rep	A knife yes. That's the kind of sharpener you'd use.	e / com
Boundary	All right ∧	m	FRAME				
Boundary	Now then ∧	m	FRAME				
Elicit	Last week we talked about all sorts of things, we talked about this picture. What did we call this this picture?	s / el		Piece of paper.	rep	A piece of paper yes.	e
Elicit	What did we call this?	el		Metal.	rep	A piece of metal yes.	e

Exchange Type	Opening	Act	Answering	Act	Follow-up	Act
Elicit	What did we call this?	el	A piece of wood.	rep	A piece of wood.	e
Elicit	What name did we give these three?	el	(INAUDIBLE)	rep		
Elicit	What name did we give these three? NV Abdul.	el b n	Materials.	rep	Good boy two team points yes. We called these materials.	e com
Elicit	What name do you think we could give to the card, the metal or the wire, the bit of wood, little bit of wool, little bit of plastic, the little bit of metal? What names can we give to all these things?	s el	Materials.	rep	Materials.	e
Repeat	What are they?	l	Materials (CHORUS)	rep	Materials.	e
Boundary	Now ∧ FRAME	m				
	Let me test your brains let me see if you can think of the materials that I'm going to ask you about. FOCUS	ms				

Elicit	If your mummy was going to make a frock, what material would she use? Hands up. NV Marie.	el cu b n	Cloth.	rep	Cloth good girl.	e
Elicit	If your mum was going to make a cardigan or a jumper what material would she use?	el	Wool.	rep	Wool good girl.	e
Elicit	If your dad was going to make a cupboard, what material would he use?	el	Wood. (CHORUS)	rep	Wood yes.	e
Elicit	If your dad was going to have a suit made, what material would the tailor use?	el	Cloth.	rep	Cloth fine yes.	e
Elicit	If your mum was going to make a cake, what material would she use?	el	$\emptyset$			
Elicit	She was going to make a cake. Yes.	el n	(INAUDIBLE)	rep		
Elicit	What material would you use for a cake?	el	—Flour—	rep	Yes you'd use flour.	e

Exchange Type	Opening	Act	Answering	Act	Follow-up	Act
Elicit	What else would you use?	el	Icing. Icing.	rep rep		
Re-Initiate	Can't hear you if you shout out.	cu	Eggs.	rep	Eggs well done Trevor.	e
Elicit	Flour and eggs and what else what other materials?	el	—Butter. Water. Sugar.	rep rep rep	Butter and sugar find, that's good yes. Eggs flour butter and sugar you'd have all sorts of things like that.	e com
Boundary	Good ∧ FRAME	m				
Boundary	Now ∧ FRAME	m				
	I'm going to give you FOCUS one of these cards.	ms				
Direct	Make sure you get one.	d				
Direct	Put it in front of you the right way up.	d				

Direct	You two can turn round. (PAUSE 5 SECONDS)	d	NV	rea
P-Elicit	Sir. Sir. Can I go to the toilet?	b b el	∅	
P-Elicit	(INAUDIBLE)	el	Yes. If you've got a printed one you shouldn't have.	rep com
P-Elicit	Sir, can I go to the toilet?	el⟨n⟩	∅	
P-Elicit	Please can I go to the toilet?	el	Climb over that way.	rep
Direct	Now er Let me see. Carys, you come and get some for your lot.	m z d⟨n⟩	NV	rea
Direct	Take that for your lot.	d	NV	rea
Direct	Turn round, David.	d⟨n⟩	NV	rea
Direct	Look at your card everyone.	d	NV	rea
Direct	Put your finger put your finger on the material we called wood.	d	NV	rea

Exchange Type	Opening	Act	Answering	Act	Follow-up	Act
Direct	Put your card flat on the desk please flat on the desk.	d	NV	rea		
Direct	Finger on the material we call wood.	d	NV	rea		
Boundary	Now∧ FRAME	m				
Elicit	Hands up. What can you see, what is the name of the cutter underneath the wood, the name of the cutter underneath the wood?	cu el	Ø			
Direct	You can't tell me because you're not looking at it.	d	NV	rea		
Elicit	The name of the cutter underneath the wood.	el	Axe.	rep	An axe yes an axe.	e
Direct	Look at the picture again and put your finger on the scissors.	d	NV	rea		
Elicit	What is the name of the material above the scissors? NV Stephen.	el b n	Paper.	rep	Paper.	e

Direct	Look at the hacksaw put your finger on the hacksaw.	d	NV	rea		
Elicit	What is the name of the thing underneath underneath the hacksaw?	el	A nut and bolt.	rep	A nut and bolt yes.	e
Direct	Look at the bottom line.	d	NV	rea		
Elicit	And erm, Ricky, you say what those three pictures are on the bottom line?	el⟨n⟩	Fasteners.	rep	Yes. [1 −]	acc
Elicit	What's the name for each one of these?	el	Paper clip.	rep	Paper clip. [3]	acc
Listing			Nail.	rep	Nail. [3]	acc
Listing			Nut and bolt.	rep	Nut and bolt. [1 +]	e
Elicit	And the name for that group?	el	Joiners. Fasteners. Fasteners.	rep rep rep	Fasteners, good.	e
Boundary	Good ∧	m FRAME				
Direct	Look at the blackboard everyone.	d	NV	rea		

Exchange Type	Opening	Act	Answering	Act	Follow-up	Act
Elicit	Here I have a paper clip and here I have the nail and here I have the nut and bolt. What do we call those three?	s el	Fasteners.	rep	Fasteners yes.	e
Direct	Look at the middle line please.	d	NV	rea		
Elicit	What do we call that line?	el	Cutters.	rep	Cutters yes.	e
Elicit	What's the name of this cutter? Hands up.	el cu	Axe.	rep	The axe the axe. And I'll put that one there.	e z
Elicit	What's the name of this cutter? Hands up. NV Janet.	el cu b n	Hacksaw.	rep	The hacksaw. And I'll put that one there.	e z
Elicit	What's the name of this cutter? Hands up. NV Yes.	el cu b n	Scissors.	rep	Scissors. I'll put that one there.	e z
Boundary	Right ˄ FRAME	m				

Direct	Now look at the cards. Point to a cutter that has some word . . .	m s d		

END OF RECORDING

5 RECENT DEVELOPMENTS

In describing work in progress, it is difficult to make clear-cut statements and it must be apparent from Chapters 3 and 4 that the most we can claim is to have begun to evolve one possible approach to the analysis of spoken texts, while working with a relatively small data sample taken from one situation type. At the same time, we are hopeful that our efforts to provide a systematic account of samples of spoken language from a small number of classrooms will be of use to others with similar interests, and stimulate further empirical studies, both in educational and other contexts. Although we would stress the preliminary nature of this work, we are confident that sufficient progress has been made for more ambitious studies to be successfully undertaken.

Our system of analysis was designed to handle discourse produced in one type of classroom situation, although we have since discovered that with minor modifications it can handle a wide range of classroom situations. As the end of the research project approached we faced the choice of continuing to work within the field of education by examining and contrasting other teaching situations, or moving outside the classroom to investigate other types of discourse.

APPLICATIONS IN EDUCATION

Within the educational field future research could have focused on the effect on classroom discourse of such variables as pupils' age, intelligence, social background, teachers' personality, size of class, subject matter, type of activity, educational level. Some of the major areas of possible investigation are outlined below.

(a) When we made our first recordings we were struck by the well-ordered nature of the texts. This was put down to the fact that the teachers, having heard our worries about making decent recordings, made a special effort to this end. However, other recordings supplied to the project showed a similar tendency towards the production of a highly organized text. In the second year of the project, we were lucky enough to receive text H, in which a teacher was simultaneously giving a lesson in the classification of objects as members of categories and also rules for making appropriate contributions to the discourse. 'Shouting out' or 'calling out' was proscribed even when the answer was correct. Pupils who made an answering move when a preliminary bid followed by a teacher nomination was required, were told 'Can't hear you if you shout out'. The importance of this example is that it shows how linguistic and social behaviour are linked, although as usual we are only aware of this when something goes wrong. In this instance, learning to speak and learning to behave are inseparable, and the discourse acts that we have identified as *cue*, *directive*, and *evaluation* show how this particular teacher instructs his eight-year-olds in making appropriate contributions to the discourse in a way that is apparently unnecessary in the recordings we have of the same teacher working with ten- and eleven-year-olds. A study of teacher-pupil interactions in the reception classes of junior schools and nursery schools could shed more light on what the rules for discourse are, as well as how they are established and learned. How does the five-year-old who speaks when he wants to become the ten-year-old who waits to be nominated?

(b) The research work to date shows a fair degree of rigidity in the framework within which teachers and pupils interact, and further work would provide teachers and teacher trainers with a powerful tool to analyse teacher styles and support judgements of teacher effectiveness. One finding of the present research is that well-planned lessons which progress in well-ordered steps to a conclusion are not necessarily successful. There are techniques, almost always used unconsciously by the teacher, which provide children with strong clues to the answer required:

Wouldn't you agree that . . .

As teachers usually take correct answers as an indication that pupils are following and understanding, any evidence that this is not true is of vital importance and has far-reaching consequences. Research of this kind would eventually provide a linguistic portrait of the classroom and permit a much more justifiable and detailed commentary on teaching behaviour.

(c) Of special interest to many teachers would be studies of interaction within groups of children when teachers are not present, and in control of the discourse. An initial difficulty would be that a teacher or other adult would presumably have to establish what was to be talked about; however, this might gradually be dispensed with, and it would be interesting to see how, over a fairly long period, pupils themselves evolved patterns of interaction and also how these might compare with teacher-pupil interactions.

(d) A cross-cultural comparison of teacher-pupil interactions involving selected schools in Britain and a country from which large numbers of immigrants have come could give some idea of whatever differences there may be between the expectations and norms that govern teacher-pupil interactions in different cultural groups. With the growing size of the immigrant population from Commonwealth countries, there is an urgent need for teachers and educational administrators in this country to be more aware of such differences where these exist. The information from such a study would not only be of intrinsic interest to cultural anthropologists; it would make a useful contribution to the resources of the educational planners and teachers who are responsible for the education of immigrant children. Moreover, it needs to be emphasized that a common language system is no guarantee that the rules for its use will be constant from one cultural or social group to another.

(e) A further question raised by this study is how far different educational levels anticipate different types of discourse. If different levels require a different type of interaction from the participants, such knowledge would be extremely useful. Studies of the ways in which discourse is ordered, say, in the first year of different secondary schools, colleges, or universities would be parallel to the study of first year secondary pupils made by Barnes and his colleagues (Barnes *et al.* 1969), with the difference that the emphasis would be on the textual pattern of the interactions, rather than the difficulties resulting from a special register of secondary education or from the use of a specialized vocabulary.

The attractions of educational research are considerable and we are happy that colleagues more intimately concerned with teaching and teacher training have begun to apply the system in teaching situations. We ourselves chose to examine other situations to discover how far the system we had developed was capable of generalization to other situations and how far it was classroom-specific.

CONTINUING WORK IN THE ANALYSIS OF DISCOURSE

Our current work, supported by the Social Science Research Council as *The Structure of Verbal Interaction in Selected Situations*, attempts to fill out and generalize the descriptive system by focusing on situations which differ in potentially important ways from the classroom. There seemed to us five major dimensions along which situations could vary.

(a) *Number and grouping of participants* The classroom has a participant structure, describable in terms of turns to speak, of one to many. On this dimension maintaining the binary grouping one could have a many-to-one situation as for example in a job interview, a many-to-many situation as in a union/management wage negotiation or a one-to-one as in a doctor/patient interview: other situations obviously have much more complex grouping and desultory conversation often has as many speaker groups as speakers.

(b) *Control* Inside the classroom the single speaker is in control of the many—he decides who will talk, what they will talk about and also acts as residual speaker, the person who is seen as responsible for dealing with silence. Control can vary in intensity, for instance in the job interview control rests with the many but the interviewee has many more rights than the pupil, even in so simple a fact as that he is allowed to talk at length and until he has finished. In doctor/patient interviews and broadcast interviews, doctor and interviewer are nominally in control of what is talked about but patient and interviewee can subtly change focus and direction.

(c) *Copresence* Most verbal interaction occurs in face-to-face situations but there are for instance telephone conversations and 'phone-in' media programmes where participants cannot see each other. Their total reliance on verbal communication means that these situations highlight such features as how interactions begin and end and various specialized techniques for exploiting both language and situation.

(d) *Intended audience* Most verbal interaction is private in the sense that it is intended solely for the participants but there are situations where the speaker is conscious of two audiences, the one that is verbally interacting with him, and the one that is

115

listening in to the situation. It is arguable that as soon as one puts a tape recorder into a situation it is no longer strictly private, but private situations can still be distinguished from public ones according to intention, whether the interaction is directly aimed at a second audience. In media discussions for example one of the functions of the chairman is to clarify for the audience references made by the participants which may not be readily understandable by the audience. The effect of the audience on the interaction and the way in which the participants take notice of the audience are obviously highly complex questions and at the moment we are not sure how to begin to answer them.

(e) *Purpose* Obviously no interactions have a single purpose, and one can categorize differences as grossly or delicately as one wishes, but we find a four-fold categorization useful—into information transmission (as in a teaching situation), fact-finding (as in parts of doctor/patient interviews), persuasion (as in a selling situation or, at times, in a courtroom), and discussion (which can be relatively focused, as in wage negotiations, or unfocused, as in media discussions).

The contrastive situations we eventually chose to work on were doctor/patient interviews, media discussions, and committees. Doctors talk to patients in private, in a one-to-one situation, with the roles clearly differentiated. The doctor is nominally in control but the purpose of the interview allows the patient to contribute structurally to the discourse. Media discussions are groupings of participants around a chairman, and with an unseen audience, and often a studio audience as well. There are often sub-groupings of participants (e.g. consumers and capitalists), and the purpose of the meeting is variable, but not normally decision-making. Committee meetings, usually held in private, are also grouped around a chairman and have various sub-groupings (e.g. unions and management). But they can have a more formal structure and agenda and often are devoted to the making of decisions.

This range was supplemented by an MA thesis on one-to-one radio interviews (Pearce 1973). These four situations obviously threw up idiosyncratic problems but the general approach has been the same and will be exemplified by reference to the work by Pearce. His thesis proposes a descriptive model developing the sort of analysis described in Chapter 3 to apply to interviews broadcast on radio and television. In extending this type of description to another situation, one of the dangers is that of forcing data into the categories set up for the description of classroom discourse; the descriptive system for the interview was therefore constructed from scratch, following the same basic principles, but taking similar analytical decisions to those in the classroom research only when supported by the interview data.

Having found that a basic analysis into sequences of Initiation–Response–Feedback was inappropriate, alternative structures were considered. The crudest analysis of broadcast interviews would recognize an interview as consisting of alternating questions and answers. However, there are a number of factors which this account fails to deal with. Firstly, for example, alalthough the term 'question' is a discourse term, in that it focuses on the intended function of an utterance in a sequence of utterances, this does not explain how the category of question is related to the grammatical category of interrogative. Secondly, it was felt that a descriptive system must be able to recognize that an utterance which functions as a question has a distinct structure of its own. Thirdly, the concept of a purely linear sequence of questions and answers obscured the fact that an interview is usually divided by linguistic means into a number of distinct episodes.

Consequently, a rank-system was eventually adopted which demonstrates that the discourse of interviews displays structural complexity similar to that of the classroom although it is restricted as to function and focus. The range of typical exchange structures is far narrower in the interview than in the classroom; for instance, interviewers do not simply give information to the respondent and so there is no interviewing equivalent of the informing exchange. Again, in the interview there are no exchanges directed at producing non-verbal responses, in contrast with the way that teachers instruct pupils to open their books, close doors and so on.

The system identifies a typical four-part exchange in the central part of the interview. Initiation and Response are seen as compulsory components, each of which may be preceded optionally by a move termed *preparatory*. Identification of the latter is based on a more systematic consideration of the structure of utterances in themselves; speech acts assigned to preparatory moves are in general those which refer directly to the previous utterance and those which indicate a speaker's willingness to contribute. An important point here is that the speakers have different rights in preparatory moves; the interviewer, for instance, cannot *evaluate* the respondent's utterance, although he can *accept* it as a complete answer.

One aspect of spoken interaction which was not important in the classroom seemed of far greater significance in the interview situation. This was that the respondent typically produced long monologues as responses. It was noticed that such monologues often contained internal structuring elements which appeared in some way to parallel the structural features of the interaction; there were, for example, features corresponding to *Focus*, such as 'I'd just like to make two points in response to that . . .' and so on. To account for the internal structuring of monologue, Pearce suggests that a separate mode of discourse be recognized here, and participants may be thought of as switching into it at certain points. Such monologue is held to be not interactionally functional in the same way as other components of interaction are. The monologue mode is incompletely examined, but the existence of certain structural features which seem to parallel the organization of interactive discourse are taken as grounds for a tentative suggestion that it would be fruitful to consider monologue as a form of projected discourse.

A further development of this type of analysis involves the recognition that a small number of surface features of discourse are used by the interviewer to give the interaction the appearance of being well-structured and having smoothness and quasi-logical sequence. A system of *chaining* features is proposed in which the use by the interviewer of words such as 'but' and 'so', pronominal anaphora and so on are explained as being systematically employed to give the interaction a surface unity and wholeness of function and development.

PRACTICE AND THEORY

In the study of each new situation the theory changes and develops. This final section discusses some aspects of our theoretical position. It is in three parts.

1. *Operational*—an account of the main hypotheses that informed the first stages, but only became explicit after they had been in use for some time.
2. Formal (linguistic)—a sketch of the concept of *latent patterning*, borrowed from literary stylistics.

3. Sociolinguistic—notes towards an appropriate *model for discourse*.

Any description of data puts to the test some abstract notions, and the more detailed and coherent the notions, the more informative is the description both where it succeeds, and where it fails. However, during 1966–70, the gestation period of this work, there was little accepted theory to build on.

The method that evolved was to construct a flexible set of loosely-related hypotheses, and to test more tentative guesses from that basis. Some of the guesses were supported by the drift of the evidence, and thereafter jostled for position among the other hypotheses. The main lines of our operational hypotheses were hammered out in research seminars and represent the sort of compromise with theory that is necessary to allow the work to continue.

1. Operational

Much of the basic argument is by analogy from syntax and phonology. It seems likely that the sources of meaning in discourse are of the same general type as those of other levels of language organization, especially levels that have been explored with academic rigour over many years. We were suspicious of structural proposals that had no parallel elsewhere in linguistics. Consequently we anticipated elementary notions like *structure* itself, like the contrast between open and closed classes, and various in-between states.

On the other hand, we were conscious of the dangers of pressing the analogy too far. In proposing discourse as an additional level of language patterning, there is an implication that some meaningful patterning will be distinctively different. Just as syntax, as against phonology, requires the notion of open classes as a necessary part of the theoretical apparatus, the next level up may have to recognize new sorts of patterning.

An important example of this novelty is the nature of sequential rules in discourse. Syntax strives towards defining the basic eligibility, or grammaticalness, of a sequence and assumes a sharp distinction between sheep and goats. Recent work on the margins of a speaker's intuitions serves only to emphasize the importance attached to this area (Quirk and Greenbaum 1972, Thorne 1973).

We found that we could not muster the same sort of intuitive sensitivity to sequences composed of utterances by different speakers. There were plenty of instances of what seemed to be oddities in the sequencing, and also some close-fitting runs, and all sorts of structures in between. But it was not possible to take over the linguistic distinction between competence and performance in any terms similar to its characteristic use in syntax.

In contrast we found a notion of *continuous classification* more readily applicable to the data. While not denying the likelihood of Todorovian macrostructures, we prefer to concentrate on the notion that the meaning of an utterance is its predictive assessment of what follows. For example, we would argue that anything following a question is to be classified in terms of the presuppositions of that question—a neatly fitting answer is only one of many natural responses, and we saw no reason to elevate it above the rest. (This point is elaborated in part 3.)

Of course, just as an individual's grammatical competence can hardly fail to be influenced by the countless millions of man-years that have been put into the teaching of English grammar, it is possible that the experience of studying discourse may sharpen one's intuitions. But the drift of our evidence is still against the likelihood of a useful concept of well-formedness in discourse, above the smallest units.

The shadowy syntactic unit *sentence* is worth consideration; never adequately defined even in written language (Fries 1957), it is capable of wide stylistic variation, and seems virtually irrelevant in speech. Nevertheless, it seems to be an essential linguistic concept. If it was a conventional unit of syntax we would expect to feel the sharp edge of grammaticalness as we encountered sentence after sentence in speech and writing. Successive clauses pass or fail the test, but sentences in some sense have to be accepted without judgement, and decoded according to a continuous classification technique. The sentence is a unit of discourse—hence its great importance, and its traditional place as a watershed in any scale of units.

Since the sentence is a unit of written discourse, similar to the *move* in speech, it will not be further elaborated here. Suffice it to say that sentence stops are perhaps best regarded as the supposed points of interaction in writing, and hence have a *tactical* element about them as well as a purely grammatical one.

It is appropriate here to consider some principles which we have taken as 'acts of faith'. Language in its interactive mode—language in use—is not necessarily best described as if its linguistic structure (as conventionally laid out) were the basic organization of the signals. The meaningful contrasts of discourse will be realized in texts by distinctions in syntax, lexis and phonology, but the ordering of these contrasts is not predictable from the lower levels. To begin with, we regarded the normal displays of language patterning as repositories of usable distinctions, but did not feel obliged to honour the ordering or the meaning of the distinctions. However, the effects of many years' training makes it difficult to ignore traditionally meaningful contrasts. For example, it is fairly easy to see that 'Aren't you coming?' is not the negative of 'Are you coming?', but rather a question with different presuppositions; it is far less easy to grasp that 'yes' and 'no' rarely contrast.

In a hierarchy of linguistic levels, there is a relation of exponence between one level and the next below. Phonology serves the exponence needs of syntax, and there is no necessary or predictable relationship between a set of phonological contrasts and a set of syntactic contrasts realized through phonology. An inventory of phonemes, and choices of stress and tone, serve basically to identify the raw material of syntactic exponence. Similarly, the exponents of, say, verb tense and number in English do not form a phonological system. The phoneme /s/ is related to other phonemes along dimensions like vowel/consonant and syllabic position. Its allophones are described in terms of their phonological environment. In contrast, one of the {s} morphemes is related to other morphemes along dimensions like past/present, singular/plural, verb class.

The uppermost level in a hierarchy cannot pass any of its descriptive problems upwards. Even if its categories are not really capable of describing the whole of linguistic meaning it has to muddle along. A reasonable symptom of the need to establish a further level would be the clustering of descriptive features in the larger structures of the uppermost level. The ceiling enforced by the design of the model would cause the description to spread out 'horizontally'.

The recent progress of work in syntax suggests that an artificial ceiling has been reached. The clause, or the sentence, has had to cope with most of the interesting complexities that research has brought to light. It now has to manage intricacies of intonation selection, information organization, semantic structuring, sociolinguistic sensitivity, illocution, and presupposition in addition to its traditional concerns. As long as no higher units or levels are proposed there is no alternative, but many of the features mentioned above are unlikely candidates for exhaustive

121

and satisfying description within clause structure.

There is plenty of evidence for structures above the sentence, but the status of the higher units has been in doubt. A simple upwards extension of syntactic categories rings false even at sentence structure, making unlikely the establishment of units akin to paragraph within syntax. And spoken language adds the phenomena of interaction, whereby a structure emerges from the utterances of more than one speaker.

The linguistic scale of *deep/surface* has been created to try to contain all this complexity. It is a sufficiently elastic concept, but it was set up to describe phenomena *within* sentences, and is not suitable for anything else. If used to tackle suprasentential patterns, it will only describe the syntactic realizations of these. The problem is akin to the description of syntactic patterns using only phonological categories—no wonder it has become so complicated!

There seems to be agreement among linguists that each meaningful contrast or selection has to be precisely located in a formal system. One place only is chosen, and from that place stems an exponence chain that can of course lead to multiple exponence, combination with other choices, deletion etc. Among considerations affecting the location of a choice, an important one is that a choice is normally held to operate in the largest unit which it influences. As that unit is broken down in analysis, or developed in generation, aspects of the selections made earlier will reappear and be described, but redundantly with respect to the selections themselves. So, for example, the passive voice of the English verb is normally assigned to clauses because it affects the selection of subjects and objects. It also shows in the construction of verbal groups, being the inclusion of (*be* + *en*), and in the words that make up those groups, but below clause structure these phenomena are simply the realizations of the choice *passive*. Maybe in due course some of its sphere of relevance will be located in discourse *illocution*, where it will be seen as one method of adjusting the sequential presentation of information in the sentence and beyond.

If in general we are to look for the fullest extent of influence of a meaningful selection, there is clear pressure from within language structure to postulate higher units. In the loose and provisional rank-scale of units that we propose for discourse, we follow certain conventions that are no more than reasonable working rules, at present.

(a) The structure at each rank will not be very complex. As soon as a rank contains structures with more than six or so elements we look for evidence of an intervening rank, by analogy with syntax and phonology.

(b) Each rank is likely to describe homogeneous patterning, so that we are to some extent using evaluative criteria. Just as clause structure in syntax deals essentially with propositional relationships, so our rank of *move* is concerned centrally with each discrete contribution to a discussion made by one speaker. We resist recognizing as a move a structure in which more than one speaker contributes, since that is more typical of the next rank up, *exchange*; but in certain circumstances (see p. 46) we are aware of conflicting criteria.

(c) The concept of rankshift, or the predictable embedding of structures at a lower rank than their place in the hierarchy suggests, is avoided as far as possible. The reasons are twofold:

(i) Rankshift remains a theoretical embarrassment, despite defences of it (Halliday 1966). Unless kept to a minimum in any descriptive framework, it destroys the framework. It is in fact a last resort.

(ii) Embedding implies discontinuity. In discourse this means that one or more participants will recognize the embedding and retrieve the original structure afterwards. When one is tempted towards this descriptive device—when for example a speaker returns to an unanswered question or a topic left hanging—there is a conflict of evidence. In such cases we choose a non-embedding method of description, although we are aware that this is a matter of operational expediency, and there are very important problems in the lack of match between, roughly, content and structure.

One major problem is the variety of different styles of discourse within one general type like 'classroom talk'. Within classroom discourse, we refer to differences between one specimen lesson and another; in the contrastive descriptions that we are now undertaking, the difficulties become more acute. In proposing distinctions between one kind of discourse and another, or between one teacher style and another, one is recognizing that descriptive categories are not necessarily transferable. It is possible in theory for two discourse types to contain no common category, and indeed the onus is upon the linguist to argue for any overlap of categories, having divided the styles initially.

The touchstone is function and not formal identification, but there is room for a variety of attitudes on what constitutes similarity. In this research we are compiling a list of features associated with what appears to be the same function and studying them, but in a slightly different fashion from the methods in syntax. In syntax it is usually possible to find a crucial criterion, or a set of such based on diagnostic procedures of deletion, addition, permutation, and commutation; in discourse the criteria are not so clear-cut.

Let us take a brief illustrative example from desultory conversation:

It's nice and warm in here, if you'd like to come through.

Superficially a statement, the descriptive problem here starts with the 'if' clause, which does not seem to indicate a condition in the main clause. A substantial number of 'if' clauses in conversation show the same phenomenon. This example appears to be a suggestion, or recommendation, made non-committally, roughly paraphrasable as:

I suggest you come through, because it's nice and warm in here.

Perhaps in due course a move called *suggestion*, with clear criteria, will be proposed. If so, one possible realization of suggestion will be:

It's nice and warm in here.

without the tell-tale if-clause. Intonation choices apart (and these are not by any means decisive), there is little to go on by way of formal clues to distinguish what could be a polite remark from a suggestion, and of course in some circumstances, the clause might be a warning of impending suffocation! Disambiguation may depend on irretrievable details of shared experience.

The existence of an apparently basic set of functions—question, answer, statement, etc.—may tempt one to fall back on these if no evidence can be found to support one's intuition. But the 'basic' functions are only a half-way house between syntax proper and discourse proper, and the example above remains ambiguous as between an informing move and a suggestion.

A similar problem exists in syntax but because of our long familiarity with conventional syntax we may not notice it so obviously. The word 'grey' in 'a grey building' is readily analysed as a colour adjective, although there are many other classes of modifier that can appear between article and noun. One short-circuits the syntax by a direct appeal to semantics. The syntactic demonstration of the class to which 'grey' belongs is only established in a rare complex nominal group like 'a fine old grey medieval building' where—participles apart—only colour adjectives can commute with 'grey'.

The search in discourse analysis is for a set of *associated features* in relation to each category, which are able to play a different role in different styles. The same feature may be confirmatory in one style, defining in another, and the touchstone of a criterion test in a third. In this way the gulf may be bridged between intuition and evidence.

Our description of classroom language says little about different styles and very little about comparative discourse types. Its definitions are thus normative because the corpus is sufficiently homogeneous to support such an approach, which of course must be abandoned as soon as substantial sociolinguistic variables are allowed to vary.

2. Latent patterning

All instances of human language are specialized forms of the notion 'I am communicating with you'—indeed some utterances are initially unspecified, and serve to indicate little more than the simple notion 'I am communicating with you'. These are commonly labelled *phatic*. Many linguists, anthropologists and others have made this point, and it is a valuable starting-point for an excursion towards an adequate linguistic theory for discourse.

We can peel the onion roughly as follows:

(a) Some features of utterances are understood to be beyond the immediate control of the speaker/writer. Abercrombie (1967) calls them *indexical*—features of voice quality, regional accent and the like. Also in this category would be distinctive statistical tendencies in a text, such as are the data of Morton's early authorship studies. The notion here is 'I can't help communicating with you'. When an individual is constructing utterances, he pays attention to getting an utterance which will be well-turned and effective. Many aspects of his pronunciation will thus be subject to constant variation within a finely meshed control structure. However those aspects of pronunciation that are not primarily concerned in the distinction of meanings may simply be carried over from one utterance to the next. If one has deliberately altered one's speech by elocution or the pressures of social mobility, then there may be further niceties of accent to control. Again, in style it is commonplace to monitor one's mannerisms and edit one's texts, sometimes to a considerable extent. But it is probably not possible to dodge a computer bent on authorship tracing, mainly because we are unaware of the statistical structure of the texts we write.

(b) Some features of utterances demonstrate patterns of un-expected regularity or irregularity. ('Unexpected' here refers to the expectations of (c) below.) Because unexpected, these patterns are not associated with established units of meaning, and their effect is heavily dependent on their context. They are called here *latent*, for reasons advanced later. The notion here is 'I am en-gaged in some sort of highly organized communication, but you have to work out for yourself what I mean.'

(c) Some features of utterances are understood with reference to systematic choices that linguists infer from their intuition and their study of texts. The actual features are not initially given a local face value but are taken to be indications of a precise route through a highly complex network, at each node of which units of meaning accrue, and the units of meaning can in principle be accurately defined. So the absence of features is just as important as the presence of them, and the resulting patterns have a stable, *recognized* meaning in the structure of the language. The notion here is, for example:

> My information focus is a certain domestic feline quadruped that you will be able to identify positively, which at a point in time remote from the moment of this utterance had adopted a posture of lowered buttocks on a small piece of floor covering of regular dimensions, which you will also be able to identify positively.

This section contrasts types (b) and (c).

The available contrasts and choices in a language are never fully exploited in that part of the structure of the language which is regularly described, and which is commonly taken to be the 'meaning-bearing' area of language patterning (type (c)). Most of the rest—what at first sight may appear to be random, acci-dental, uncontrolled—are relegated to the dim province of stylistic variation, or not mentioned at all. These are of type (b).

Some notice has to be taken of them in the careful study of literary texts, advertising language, oratory and other varieties which have developed additional conventions that invest them with ancillary meaning.

Few could quarrel with the distinction between the recognized patterns and the latent patterns, and the half-way house of stylistic patterns. The failure of linguistics is that it has concentrated in its theoretical development solely on the recognized patterns.

The job of describing latent patterns is not simply an extension of the usual apparatus into greater delicacy, or greater comprehensiveness. The distinction between the two major types is sound and the one cannot be absorbed into the other, even if it turns out that there is a continuum between the extremes of, say, the function of initial *s* and final *s* in English nouns. Initial *s* is a phoneme and serves the purpose of helping the noun to be identified. Final *s* can be the realization of the plural morpheme, and in that case shows a recognized pattern. But initial *s* can also carry the latent pattern of alliteration, where there is no fixed unit of meaning to accrue. (Final *s* can of course participate in latent patterning too.)

A trivial example will make the point. If all available patterning could be assigned a recognized meaning, then the descriptive apparatus would have to be non-finite because there can be no upper limit fixed on the extent of a unit that can carry latent patterns. All possible combinations of all possible features up to a certain rank, like sentence, would be fairly formidable as a starting-point. But if there is no upward limit we would never know whether or not there were further regularities lying outside the maximum span of the moment. So the apparatus to be devised must be different in kind from that used for recognized patterns.

Latent patterns are only optional in the sense that they can be effectively avoided. Avoidance is just as positive a task for a speaker or writer as exploitation, and textbooks on 'Better Writing' are at pains to teach avoidance of latent patterns. 'Elegant variation' is another prescriptive technique for avoiding one sort of latent patterns.

At this point we distinguish three important types of latent pattern, in order to focus the discussion.

1. Those which create further local meaningful choices, not anticipated in descriptions of recognized patterns. These range from familiar rhetorical figures and prosodies to *ad hoc* subtle-

127

ties of literary ambiguity. Among the figures are all kinds of antithesis and syntactic parallelism; and their prosodic counterparts such as alliteration, rhyme and assonance. This paper is not an appropriate forum for further consideration of them (see Sinclair 1972).

2. Those which require a reclassification of recognized patterns for their description. In the course of normal syntactic generalization one puts together items which are different and separates items which are the same. It is held that there are half a dozen 'different' verbs *be* in English (exponents of modal—*is to*, future—*is going to*, continuous, passive, existential, equational, not to mention idiomatic uses). Yet there are grounds for suspecting that the occurrence of any of them in a question has a constant effect upon the presuppositions of that question.

Still on verbs, the imperative, base form, to-infinitive, 3rd plural present, 1st and 2nd present, are distinct in an analysis of recognized patterns, but in appearance are all identical. Their identity—a latent pattern—makes it possible for an enormous variety of instructions to have a common, quasi-imperative form, e.g.

	sit	down now
I want you to	sit	down now
please	sit	down now
let's	sit	down now
would you	sit	down now
sensible people	sit	down now[1]
you	sit	down now

3. Those which actually carry meaning but are not recognized in descriptions because they realize choices at the level of discourse. One major effect of establishing discourse as a linguistic level is the transfer of these patterns from latent to recognized; conversely one major reason for proposing discourse as an additional level is the wish to recognize some latent patterns as regularly meaning-bearing but not describable in syntactic or semantic terms.

Linguists have been doing sentence-grammar for so long, and devising ingenious ways of coping with the 'ceiling' effect described above, that they are unlikely to welcome the suggestion of transferring some syntactic features to discourse. Syntax and semantics must remain for them at the apex of the pyramid. Even

---

[1]cp. Gentlemen lift the seat—British Rail.

if one manages to make a case for discourse being the location of many meaningful choices, there is a danger that the meaning will be described all over again in syntax and semantics.

Here is an example to illustrate the sort of rethinking that will be required. It has been noted in descriptive grammars of English that the past tense is sometimes used when no past time reference is indicated, for example as a polite interruption:

Oh, sorry—I just wanted to check a few points.

Very often the progressive aspect is chosen.

. . . I was just wondering if you could have a look at this.

The inappropriateness of inserting a past-time adjunct, e.g. 'five minutes ago' shows that the actual time reference is to the moment of utterance.

It is part of the job of discourse analysis to identify elements of structure such as *greeting*, *initial move*, *interruption*, and to categorize utterances on scales such as formality, politeness, embarrassment. The last example could be described as

I wonder if . . . [$^+$interrupt] [$^+$transaction initial] [$^+$polite]

The syntax is then free to ignore this oddity of past tense usage.

Of course the option is open to extend the feature list and abbreviate the sentence still further. 'I wonder if you could' is a so-called 'softener' preceding a verb base 'have', and the utterance could be analysed as

DIRECTIVE: have a look at this: [$^+$softener] [$^+$ . . . etc.]

(We have used conventions of feature analysis here purely for convenience.)

It is not yet clear what contrasts and choices should be assigned to which level, nor what the eventual impact upon syntax may be. There might well be a greater concentration upon the propositional content of utterances; the generality of syntactic statements will be more effective if many of the apparently minor uses of forms are assigned to discourse; perhaps deceptive terminology like *past* and *present* will get the final death-sentence. Part 3 (below) offers notes on the possible field of reference of the level of discourse.

3. A model for discourse

Since the model is hierarchical, we shall use a vertical analogy and talk of *height* as representing two related concepts:
(a) place of a unit in the taxonomy—a familiar use
(b) directness of relationship to recognized syntactic patterns. The deliberate ambiguity is possible because, in general, indirect categories operate in the structure of upper units in the taxonomy. We start at the top.

Orientation

At the highest stratum of all there is the interpenetration of minds. Each individual constructs his private linguistic universe, and through his utterances gives hints as to its nature. A problem which has always been with linguistics is the relation between subjective and objective ways of understanding the nature of language. Firth tried to exorcise this dichotomy along with the others, but did not succeed. But through the concept of orientation we are able to build both subjective and objective aspects into a coherent model of verbal communication.

One possibility is that participants can maintain a consistent orientation towards each other throughout an interaction. Another is that they can converge on or diverge from each other. Or their orientation may be sensitive to smaller units of the discourse and may vary considerably. Or one participant may adopt an idiosyncratic mode. Because orientation is signalled through a complex network of choices, there are many configurations.

In classroom discourse we have mainly examples of consistency. The teacher's orientation is rarely challenged. The process of education is seen as the pupils accepting the teacher's conceptual world, since he is the mouthpiece of the culture. In some lessons the quality of acceptance seems to be superficial— literally making the same noises as the teacher; as when the teacher indicates clearly the answer required and then demands a choral response of the target word or phrase.

The domination of the teacher's language is fully displayed in the earlier chapters of this book. The basic IRF structure, giving the teacher the last word, allows him to recast in his own terms any pupil response. Pupils acknowledge the domination by choosing elliptical responses, and by avoiding initiating. Programmed instruction texts often take this sort of interaction to embarrassing extremes.

In an interview between doctor and patient, there is an attempt to construct a conceptual frame compounded of what each brings to the interaction. The doctor brings his expertise in classification and diagnosis, and the patient brings his symptoms. The doctor is able to dominate, but the patient retains many subtle ways of insisting on his own view of things. One tactic is for the patient to refuse the doctor's verbal descriptions, and restate his own; the actual words shared are important. One of our examples shows a verbal tussle between doctor and patient about 'pains' in the region of the 'heart' (patient) or 'chest' (doctor). While apparently agreeing with each other, they carry on this vocabulary disagreement through several utterances.

Again, doctors often use a checking routine where they offer a formulation that the patient may quietly accept or may treat as a polar question and reopen the discussion. That is typical converging behaviour—the doctor indicating his position and inviting but not compelling the patient to accede to it. The doctor says, perhaps, 'Tight pain, yes', his intonation falling, and this in response to the same words used by the patient; the doctor has picked them out for checking.

In committee language, where talk is designed to achieve communal decisions, there can develop a power struggle that comes out very clearly in the patterns of orientation. A participant wishing to dominate will continually assert a distinctive phraseology of his own and will, in heated moments, use the words as weapons, almost regardless of their recognized meaning.

The category of orientation is a grouping of systems, which themselves are groupings of choices realized in the language. Certain tracks through the network will result in classifications similar to quite familiar everyday ones—the hostile witness, the difficult patient, the permissive teacher. Other tracks will show inconsistencies, changing relationships. The assumption is that we are forever signalling our orientation in our latent patterning, and that the most important place to look for the signals is the first few words of an utterance.

The systems that carry orientation are primarily *lexicoreferential*; for example

(a) The selection of actual words, particularly at the beginning of an utterance. A lot of echoing is a sign of convergence; the use of synonyms signals local divergence, and a lack of overlay in vocabulary indicates a general inability or refusal to enter a common universe of discourse.

(b) The use of substitution words, referring back to the previous speaker's actual words. These signal an overlapping of orientations, but the speaker retains independence.

(c) The choice of elliptical structures, one-word answers and the like; where the syntax of an utterance depends on that of the previous speaker. Acceptance of the domination of another is the meaning that emerges from this choice. Cross-examining barristers ('Answer yes or no', 'Confine yourself to answering my question') are presumably engaged in verbal bullying when they attempt to restrict the efforts of a witness to avoid domination.

Note that although orientation is the 'highest' category of discourse meaning, it is realized in rather superficial text choices. Detailed description of the realization awaits two events —the publication of Hasan on cohesion, and the mounting of a computer-based study of transcripts to test the hypotheses.

Organization

Lower than orientation is the network of choices through which participants signal their strategies for the conduct of the discourse. The two main systems relate to the placing of boundaries, and the alignment of participants within the boundaries.

Major boundaries in classroom language are signalled by Frame and Focus; other discourse types show them, sometimes less clearly. They signal such things as 'I am starting off something new now', 'I am finishing off'. Often they are role-related; that is a certain speaker is expected to assign certain boundaries. A description of minor boundaries requires a study of the organization of turn-taking and predictable interruptions. This area did not need exploration in the study of classroom language, but is a major preoccupation in current work.

The alignment of participants covers the way in which they extend, contract and vary the progress of a unit. Current unpublished work on intonation by Brazil has opened up a fascinating field of signalling based principally on the pitch of the final tone-group of an utterance. At present he proposes a system of *key* choice, with three terms (high, mid, low) whose names are a rough guide to their pitch-ranges. There is rarely a choice of all three, general progression is downwards, and there can only be one choice of mid key in a unit. A high key choice engages the other participants and opens up the unit; a mid key is detached and neutral; a low key is a closing gesture, although the unit can nevertheless be prolonged by subsequent speakers.

Fit

The category below *organization* concerns the ways in which successive items in the discourse are related. It handles the relationships described as 'adjacency pairs' by Sacks (1972) and Schegloff and Sacks (1973), the three question-types of Labov (1970), and draws on the notion advanced earlier of *continuous classification*.

Each successive utterance provides a frame of reference for whatever follows. An utterance which ends in an open elicitation, for example, can be answered (i) by a minimal, totally fitting response, or (ii) by something which satisfies the notional presuppositions of the elicitation but is structurally independent, or (iii) by something which implies an adequate answer but principally sets up further presuppositions, or (iv) by something which challenges the terms of the question—was it properly asked, was there a feasible answer, was it directed at the right addressee, etc.

A What is the capital of England?

B (i) London.
  (ii) If you look at this map, you'll see it's in big type.
  (iii) I suppose you're thinking of London, my home town.
  (iv) Why do you ask?
    That's an irrelevant question.
    I'm afraid I don't know a thing about capitals and all that.
    Good gracious, don't you know?

There are other possibilities, of course; 'beg pardon', or a complete break in the discourse, suggesting the question was misheard or is being crudely evaded.

With each discourse type is associated one or more recurrent structures; the classroom pattern of I R F is one of the clearest. If the above example was from a classroom, and the pupil gave a fully-fitting response such as (i), then the next contribution would be an evaluation of that response by the teacher.

Our work on *fit* goes back to the beginnings of the research, but progresses only slowly. Each attempt at a thorough description begs so many questions of other areas of the description, that it is regularly shelved.

Play

This category concerns the choices open to an individual at any one point in an interaction (whereas *fit* deals with the meaning produced by the interlocking of utterances). Within the range of choices and meanings prescribed by the higher categories, there are still many options, subtle variations and *ad hoc* structural modifications that can be made. To describe them, we take over the concept of *illocution* from the linguistic philosophers. For example, it was mentioned earlier that some utterances can be classified as *suggestions*, but we have at present no class of move with that name. An utterance that clearly requires some activity to satisfy its presuppositions is a *directive*, and the division of directive into all the many kinds involves a study of the illocutionary force of each. Only where there is a unique effect on the structure of exchanges are there grounds for recognizing a distinct category of move. We regard illocution as a set of choices derived from the internal structure of utterances.

Assembly

This is the lowest category, carrying practically no discourse meaning. But as the main interface between grammar and discourse it will probably emerge as the most interesting network descriptively. It would be folly to speculate in any detail about assembly systems at the present time.

The diagram opposite illustrates the relations between categories of meaning, systems of choice, units of discourse, and the surface realizations in language. As height increases, so also does the gap between the units and the categories of meaning.

In conclusion, note the following:
(a) There is a rough horizontal correspondence between the two scales in the diagram, particularly in the lower reaches where we anticipate that most discourse types will follow the same rules. Higher up there is a possibility that more units for the rank scale will be postulated, or that some discourse types will

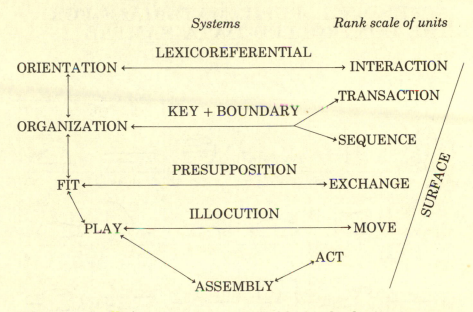

Systems   *Rank scale of units*

not require all those that are available in the language as a whole. The left-hand categories, however, are exhaustive and apply to every instance of interactive language.

(b) A converging orientation may correlate often with a closing key choice and a place of minimal presupposition with an illocutionary force that is supportive. But it is possible to manipulate the categories to provide the vast subtlety of personal social relationships that we observe in natural language. A speaker may select a diverging orientation to stand as a boundary; use high key to indicate that he expects others to be as involved and independent as he is; make his utterance a rhetorical general question so that no reply is expected, and so on, ending up with

Well, you can't win 'em all, can you?

As a final example, we shall select a neutral ritualized orientation, mid key to indicate that the normal expectations continue, presupposition that the move is a major closing boundary, and pick for assembly an idiom:

the end

APPENDIX I PUPIL MATERIALS FOR THE CONTROLLED DATA SAMPLE

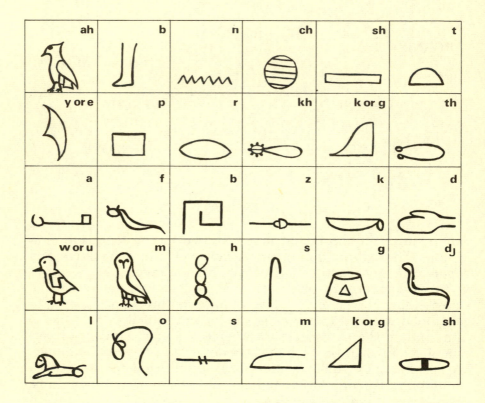

ah	b	ñ	ch	sh	t
y or e	p	r	kh	k or g	th
a	f	b	z	k	d
w or u	m	h	s	g	dj
l	o	s	m	k or g	sh

Here is a table showing some of the hieroglyphs and the sounds they represent. They were used over 2,000 years ago for religious ceremonies and business of state.

Try to decipher the hieroglyphs on the next page with the information contained in this table.

This material was prepared originally by Ian Forsyth and Kathleen Wood and is included in the first book of their English course *Communication and Language* (Longman, forthcoming).

Here are three cartouches. The names they represent are given in Greek, but you will probably recognize them as they are much the same in English. The hieroglyphs have been numbered to correspond with the left to right ordering of letters in our writing.

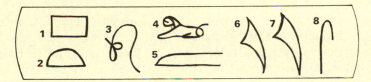

(a)   An Egyptian King

(b)   A Famous Queen

As well as referring to sounds in the language, these signs may refer to ideas, for example, in (b) numbers 10 and 11 are not to be taken as letters; they mean respectively 'divine' and 'female'.

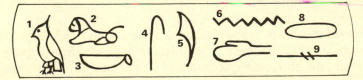

(c)   An Emperor and a Soldier

APPENDIX II   CRITICAL BIBLIOGRAPHY

Bales, R. F.
Interaction Process Analysis. Reading, Mass.: Addison Wesley, 1951

The perspective held on interaction in most classroom interaction studies is found within sociology in the work of Bales. The study of interaction is undertaken by Bales in order to develop the structural-functionalist theory of social systems. He is interested in the social cohesion of the interactive group and in types of problem-solving behaviour. All behaviour within a group is regarded as functional either to solving the task problem or to maintaining the necessary background social relations. It is in terms of these interests that Bales develops his system of analysis. Glosses on types of verbal behaviour available within the language become categories with which units of behaviour are labelled. With these categories participants are categorized as playing dominantly 'instrumental', i.e. task-oriented roles, or dominantly 'expressive', i.e. socially integrative roles. These roles emerge through quantification of occurrences of the functional units in the category system, and changing roles can be represented graphically. Bales' categories are intended to be generally applicable to all types of small group, in order that comparisons can be made of the effects on interaction of such variables as personality, social organization, culture and the type of problem and situation. Such questions as what a unit is or how participants understand the function of particular utterances or of non-verbal behaviour are not taken as centrally problematic. The observer is said to code according to the point of view of the addressee, assuming that point of view through some kind of empathic identification. Bales specifically rules out of his set of categories the question of how a series of acts relate to each other as part of a larger context. The process of interaction is viewed merely as the succession of individual functional units.

Barnes, D.
'Language in the Secondary Classroom'. In D. Barnes, J. Britton and H. Rosen, *Language, the Learner and the School.* Harmondsworth: Penguin Books, 1969

Barnes' analysis of recordings of a day of lessons of a first year comprehensive school class was undertaken to specify areas of language difficulty met by children in moving from the junior to the secondary level of education. He hypothesized that the children's difficulties would be with linguistic forms and socio-linguistic demands which were social rather than intrinsic to the material and processes being learned. The method of analysis developed was designed to indicate links between patterns of language of the teacher and patterns in the learning of the children. The categories are motivated by pedagogic concerns, and are used to develop critical and evaluative insights into teaching processes rather than for systematic description of the verbal interaction.

Bateson, G.
'Towards a Theory of Schizophrenia'. In *Behavioural Science* I, 1956, p. 251

Beginning with Bateson, one school of psychoanalysts have sought to understand the characteristic forms of behaviour and the genesis of the condition termed 'schizophrenia' in terms of the relationship of the patient with his family, or, more speci-fically, in terms of the communication patterns within the family. Symptomatic of schizophrenia is the patient's inability to judge accurately what the other means, and in turn his production of what are, for the everyday mode of interpretation, uninterpret-able and inconsequent utterances. Characteristic is a confusion of literal and metaphoric language, both in production and in reception. Bateson, drawing on Russell's theory of logical types, illustrates types of communication which involve multiple logical types. In learning to communicate we have to learn different modes of communication such as play, phantasy, metaphor. Jokes make use of a leap from one mode to another. Signals identifying a mode are capable of falsification. Bateson suggests that the individual who becomes schizophrenic has systematically been prevented from learning to discriminate between these modes by a strategy known as the 'double-blind' involving consistent falsification of mode-signalling devices. For example, paralanguage may indicate a mother's hostility towards her child, while overtly the mother expresses concern.

Bellack, A. A. *et al.*
The Language of the Classroom. New York: Teachers College Press, 1966

The focus of this research was meanings as conveyed by language used in the classroom. The teaching situation is seen as a 'game' after Wittgenstein (1953) involving a number of players. An analysis is made of transcriptions from tape-recorded lessons in terms of 'pedagogical moves', 'teaching cycles', and 'categories of meaning'. All the verbal behaviour of pupils and teachers is coded into one of four moves. Varying combinations of these moves make up 'teaching cycles'. Moves are coded also according to 'categories of meaning', to distinguish types of substantive, logical, and instructional meanings communicated. The coding was used to discover the distribution between teacher and pupils of the types of moves and meanings they carried.

Bernstein, B.
'A Sociolinguistic Approach to Socialization'. In Gumperz and Hymes (eds.), 1972

It is part of our thesis that grammatical differences *per se* between teacher and pupil are less significant than the variation in functions available to individuals in these roles, and that grammatical differences occurring are likely to be a function of the distribution of move-options. Bernstein has latterly suggested that this also appears to be the case in the relation of social class to language use. Having at first sought to correlate two distinct codes, defined by degree of grammatical elaboration characteristic within them, with users' membership of a social class (1962, 1964), in his later work he looks at types of role relationship within families, particularly types of parental control of the child, and sees grammatical differences in the ways of realizing such functions as control, as the point of articulation between language and social class.

Boyd, J., and Thorne, J. P.
'The Semantics of Modal Verbs'. In *Journal of Linguistics* vol. 5, 1969

Transformational grammar is supposed to be able to account for the deep structural similarities between sentences with different surface structures, and deep structure differences lying beneath identical surface realizations. The sentence 'You will go' can be interpreted as a command, equivalent to 'I order you to go' or as a declarative statement, so the deep grammar of this sentence ought to provide two analyses which will account for its surface ambiguity. This problem has recently led to an explicit attempt to build the 'illocutionary force' or function of sentences into deep grammar. Boyd and Thorne discuss the illocutionary force of sentences containing modal verbs, 'will', 'can', 'would', 'could', etc., and give analyses of declarative surface structures, which show that their semantic deep structure is not always that of a statement. They suggest, for example, that the modal verb 'will' is an indicator that the illocutionary potential of a sentence containing it is that of being a prediction.

Cazden, C. V. J., John, V. P., and Hymes, D. (eds.)
Functions of Language in the Classroom. New York: Teachers College Press, 1972

Only four of the papers in this collection actually study functions of language as recorded or observed in the classroom. The other papers focus on such topics as the differential norms for communication held by sub-cultural groups, but not on the effects of pupils' communicative expectations or their actual classroom behaviour and experiences. Mishler's paper does analyse tape-recorded data from a first grade classroom and demonstrates how specific forms of language indicate different cognitive strategies. From the point of view of analysing classroom discourse, several of the papers suggest possibilities for further research in the theoretically fruitful situations where interpretive discourse rules are not shared and taken for granted, and therefore are likely to be more easily recognizable by the researcher. From the point of view of discourse analysis in general the volume offers studies of a variety of situations, using a variety of analytic approaches. Horner and Gussow's paper referred to in the notes on Skinner is included in this volume.

Flanders, N. A.
Teacher Influence, Pupil Attitudes and Achievement: Studies in Interaction Analysis. Co-operative Research Monographs no. 12, U.S. Government Printing Office, 1965

Flanders is perhaps the best known and most influential analyst of classroom interaction. His methods have been used in literally hundreds of independent studies. The system of analysis comprises seven categories for teacher talk, two categories for pupil talk and a tenth category for 'silence or confusion'. Observers are present in the classroom and code verbal utterances in real time, at three-second intervals. The distribution of the categories is used to identify teaching styles according to whether they tend to be direct (teacher-centred) or indirect (pupil-centred). Flanders' system of analysis was designed not simply for descriptive purposes, but as a tool for testing hypotheses about the effects of teacher styles on pupil achievement and attitudes.

Frake, C. O.
'Struck by Speech: The Yakan Concept of Litigation'. In Gumperz and Hymes (eds.), 1972

Frake focuses on litigation as a speech situation. It is a situation defined almost wholly by the content and structure of the talk which occurs in the Yakan culture studied. There is no courtroom, no special dress to mark this situation off from other similar situations such as 'discussion', 'conference', or 'negotiation'. Each activity, however, has different components, different rules of procedure, different sequential organization. The litigation situation is composed of a sequence of twelve events—such events as the 'presentation of the case', 'testimonies', 'interrogation', and so on. Exactly how each of the events differs from the other, in terms of the actual speech sequences which make them up, is not discussed at length though some examples are given of the appropriate style and content used in making a ruling and justifying penalties imposed. The procedural rules for the conduct of litigation deal with the rights and obligations of various participants to contribute and to whom contributions must be addressed.

Gallagher, J. J., and Aschner, M. J.
'A Preliminary Report on Analyses of Classroom Interaction'. *Merrill-Palmer Quarterly*, vol. 9, 1963, pp. 183–94.

This study focuses on the relation of productive thought processes in pupils to verbal interaction in the classroom. The category system developed is for sequences of cognitive processes and includes five categories, for memory, routine, and convergent, divergent, and evaluative thinking. The data analysed consists of tape-recordings, and accompanying notes by trained observers on the general atmosphere, and the general behaviour of the teacher including his use of praise, humour, disciplinary measures, teaching materials, and so on. One finding is a clear correspondence in patterning between the thought processes of teachers and pupils, suggesting that the quality of thinking is largely dependent on the way in which the teacher structures the classroom situation.

Garfinkel, H.
Studies in Ethnomethodology. Englewood Cliffs, N.J.: Prentice Hall, 1967

The function of an utterance is normally clear and definite within its particular context. How participants to conversation rely on context in order to understand the meaning and function of utterances is a major focus of ethnomethodology, a sociological perspective initiated by Garfinkel. Garfinkel is interested in how language, and procedures made possible by language, are used to provide a sense of social order in everyday life and in the accounts of social life constructed by professionals in sociology and other disciplines. He engages in a theoretical debate with current conceptions of language meaning and function in linguistics and philosophy.

Garfinkel, H., and Sacks, H.
'On formal structures of Practical Actions'. In J. C. McKinney and E. Tiryakian (eds.) *Theoretical Sociology*, 1969

Garfinkel and Sacks discuss the conversational practice of 'formulating', i.e. 'saying in so many words what we are doing, (or what we are talking about, or who is talking, or who we are or where we are)'. 'A member may treat some part of the conversation as an occasion to describe that conversation, to explain it, or characterize it, or translate, or summarize, or furnish the gist of it, or take note of its accordance with rules, or remark on its departure from the rules.' When participants formulate what they are doing in a conversation they are attempting to be explicit, to remedy the ambiguities of talk. However, Garfinkel and Sacks argue that formulations are themselves produced and understood by glossing practices, i.e. they index their context and are understood in terms of their context. It is not therefore on formulations that participants' ability to understand, for example, what topic they are talking about, depends. This argument is supported by the observation that although there are many names for conversational activities they are little used, and can in many cases be seen as incongruous, boring, incompetent, devious, etc.

143

Goffman, E.
'The Neglected Situation'. In J. J. Gumperz and D. Hymes, *The Ethnography of Communication: American Anthropologist* part 2, 1964, p. 666

This writer within the symbolic interactionist perspective stands out for his advocacy of the study of face-to-face interaction as an autonomous topic. In many articles and books he has pointed out that interaction has its own formal structures (1961, 1963, 1967). The structure of interaction is not in itself linguistic, although it is largely through the medium of language that it is manifested. Goffman points out that interactions have to be opened and closed; it has to be ensured that attention and understanding are established, that cues are given for speakers to contribute or to cease speaking, that the interaction is proceeding normally for the purposes the encounter was designed for, and so on. Through close attention to detail he captures the features of social interaction, but his method is really a personal style of observation and comment, not usable by others as a model. Many of his observations and terms, however, have passed into sociological and sociolinguistic language and provide ways of talking about the topic we are concerned with and its constituent features.

Gumperz, J. J., and Hymes, D. (eds.)
Directions in Sociolinguistics, New York: Holt, Rinehart, Winston, 1972

This recent collection of articles is an important contribution towards defining the field of the ethnography of communication. Gumperz in his introduction makes a historical survey of the development of the field, and the volume includes comprehensive references and a critical bibliography. The papers include studies by anthropologists of non-Western cultures in which most attention is given to the uses of language over a whole encounter, more recent studies by sociologists and linguists of features of American speech and non-verbal communicative behaviour, and theoretical and methodological discussions. The focus of this volume, 'The interactional approach to language behaviour', is of course broader than that of discourse analysis on the structure of conversation.

Halliday, M. A. K.
'Language Structure and Language Function'. In J. Lyons (ed.)

New Horizons in Linguistics. Harmondsworth: Penguin Books, 1970

Halliday is concerned not with the function or meaning of a given utterance of a sentence, but rather with the function of the presence and surface ordering of elements within a sentence. His approach draws on the work of the Prague linguists, towards a synthesis of structural and functional approaches in linguistics. Halliday insists that without an examination of grammar there is no reason for making any particular classification of language uses, unless one uses 'external' psychological or sociological generalizations about the uses of language. He finds in the structure of the clause, three functions: (1) the 'ideational'—expressing content; (2) the 'interpersonal'—maintaining social relations; and (3) the 'textual'—enabling links to be made with the situation and cohesive texts to be constructed. Halliday is not dealing with these functions at a level which would enable us to analyse how long stretches of coherent interaction are organized. He discusses the textual function, providing for the coherence of clauses and sentences mainly in terms of pronominal reference. This tells us something about how in surface grammar a particular response might be expressed in order to fit with a previous sentence, but nothing about what sort of response would be appropriate and coherent after, for example, a question. Halliday's discussion of communication roles is in terms of the 'grammatical subject' of clauses, said to define the role adopted by the speaker, rather than in terms of the moves available to a participant in discourse. Halliday is interested in the use made of language in order to give principles for explaining why the structure of language is organized in one way rather than another. Linguistics for him should be centrally concerned with language use and he rejects distinctions between 'langue' and 'parole', or competence and performance. In fact his discussion of language functions is concerned with those formal features of language which enable to be expressed relations without which human communication would be impossible. Examples include the distinction between self and other, a concept of spatial relation and of temporal relation. At the very particular level of why the surface structure of a particular clause is as it is Halliday also contributes. For example, the textual component enables a speaker to use language in a way relevant to the context. One option here is thematization. In English this is effected by placing the crucial elements of a message in first place in the sentence. Attentions to such options as thematizing could provide a more delicate description of the lowest functional units we identify.

Hymes, D.
'Models of the interaction of language and social setting'. *Journal of Social Issues.* 23, 2, 1967, pp. 8–28

Since the beginning of the 1960's Hymes has attempted to outline a programme for an integrated study of language and use which he calls the 'ethnography of speaking'. Consistently he has pointed back to the interests of earlier linguists, such as Sapir, in all aspects of language, and the close links in the development of American linguistics with anthropology, severed in the interests of making linguistics an autonomous science. Hymes' programme for an ethnography of speaking suggests comprehensive studies of native systems and theories of speaking, aiming to describe the communicative competence that enables a member of a community to know when to speak and when to remain silent, which code to use, when, where and to whom. He suggests that some of the notions with which a theory of language will have to deal include speech community, speech situation, speech act, speech event, the fluent and the native speaker, components of speech events, functions of speech, rules of speaking, and types of speech event or act. Hymes points out that the aim of stating rules of speaking has as a consequence 'the inseparability of sociolinguistic analysis from the full-scale analysis of social life; for it is in the analysis of social life that the requisite rules of selection for sociolinguistic features are to be found and stated'. (1967)

Jefferson, G.
'Side Sequences'. In D. Sudnow (ed.), 1972

Jefferson discusses a type of sequence which can be seen to be a *break* in an engaging activity. It is in some sense relevant, but not a part of the activity, yet does not constitute a *termination* of the activity. This paper focuses on the questioning repeat, which requires the original speaker to talk more on the product-item before the on-going talk can be returned to. A questioning repeat generates a type of side-sequence termed a 'misapprehension-sequence'. Such a sequence is generated in accordance with a rule that if a statement (s) is made and followed by a demonstration or assertion (m) that the hearer did not understand, then the first speaker *may* or *must* provide a clarification (c). Jefferson moves on to discuss how side-sequences are built into longer sequences of discourse. A series—O, S, R—is introduced, where O is an exchange in the on-going discourse, S the interrupting side-sequence, and R the return to the on-going discourse. It is argued that side-sequences are seen by participants to be subsidiary sequences, with a promise that the on-going activity will be resumed.

Joos, M.
The Five Clocks. New York: Harbinger Books, 1962

Joos suggests five main speech styles, ranging from 'frozen' to 'intimate', each with characteristic degrees of elaboration or truncation and ellipsis of structure. These grammatical styles he relates to the type of social relationship between speakers, to their relative status and degree of acquaintance. Most important he suggests an explanation for variation in grammatical elaboration in terms of the presence or absence of opportunities for a listener to provide feedback, and its consequences for the speaker's verbal planning. The lecturer's speech is highly elaborate and redundant because listeners cannot ask for repetition or rephrasing, while the speech of intimates can be truncated, both because it relies on a wealth of common experience and shared knowledge for its interpretation, and because the listener can constantly provide feedback indicating comprehension.

Labov, W.
'The Study of Language in its Social Context'. *Studium Generale* 23, 1970, pp. 30–87

Modern linguistics has been concerned predominantly with language as an autonomous formal system, abstracted from its context of social use and considered as homogeneous over all its speakers. Its emphasis, reinforced by Chomsky, has drawn attention away from language in use, even as data for phonological and grammatical analysis. Labov in this discussion of features of American-Negro English usually treated as non-systematic free variants argues that linguistic description even at the phonological level needs to include 'variable (context-dependent) rules' which can be discovered only by the study of actual usage. Because linguistics has usually narrowed the definition of its object to exclude context dependency, fruitful though it has been, the area now designated 'sociolinguistics' has become vast, the term being frequently used for the study of anything in language that is not a feature of homogeneous structure. Labov points out in this paper that his concern is with theoretical questions within general linguistics—with phonological, morphological, and syntactic rules within a single language, which do, however, he argues, depend on context. A second area of sociolinguistics Labov suggests should be termed the 'sociology of language'—the study of the interaction of large-scale social factors with language. The third area of sociolinguistics is the functional study of language in use. Labov points to a common focus emerging here between sociolinguists, psychiatrists, and ethnomethodologists in 'the fundamental problem of discourse analysis: to show how one utterance follows another in a rational, rule-governed manner—in other words how we understand coherent discourse' (1970).

Labov, W.
'Rules for Ritual Insults'. In D. Sudnow (ed.), 1972

Labov identifies a speech activity termed 'sounding', constituted by a series of insults, which are responded to not as personal insults requiring a denial or rebuke, but as a demonstration of artistry, requiring a matching display of skill. In differentiating ritual and personal insults which generate different response sequences, Labov shows how both grammatical form and social assumptions are relied on. For a ritual insult, the form is 'A is so X, that P'. The necessary assumption is that the attribution is false and is known by speaker and hearers to be false. Labov shares the ethnomethodologists' emphasis on formulating rules for generating appropriate speech sequences (an emphasis of course drawn from structural linguistics). He also pays greater attention to the role of grammatical form, as well as common-sense knowledge, in the interpretation of utterances and provides a model example of how these two features can be considered together.

Sacks, H.
'On the analyzability of stories by children'. In Gumperz and Hymes (eds.), 1972

Sacks discusses (a) how a specific utterance is generated by an observation, i.e. with the rules that provide for what was actually said being a relevant selection from all the possible things that might have been said; (b) how we discriminate a specific sense from potentially ambiguous terms; (c) how we hear certain terms for objects (and persons) and activities as related, both within sentences and across sentences, i.e. in the latter case, with coherence above the sentence. Sacks is here concerned with one utterance by one speaker, and of a type not designed to elicit a response. Nevertheless, the concepts and rules suggested can be used, as he intends them to be, for the analysis of how several speakers interact coherently, making relevant contributions which are tied-in to previous remarks by others as well as themselves. The relationships of coherence between utterances in a discourse is dealt with, by this apparatus, mainly in terms of the development of topics. Such concepts as 'category-bounded activity' enable us to see how a remark, e.g. about a certain activity, can be an extension of a topic centring around a particular type of 'member', even though grammatically no reference is made back to any referential item.

Schegloff, E.
'Notes on a Conversational Practice: Formulating Place'. In D. Sudnow (ed.), 1972

Schegloff considers two kinds of discourse problems. One is the selection of terms to refer to places, a semantic question like the question of selecting terms for persons, but which itself requires taking account of who the recipient is. The second question is about what type of utterance properly follows a question. Schegloff shows that a sequence can be inserted between a question and its answer and be seen to be a relevant pre-sequence to the answer, rather than for example an evasion. One kind of relevant pre-sequence to giving an answer involving 'direction-giving' involves establishing information necessary to give a proper place formulation in the answer. That is, questions of how one makes reference are also involved in seeing a series of utterances as a 'proper' sequence, and a sequence of a particular structure.

Searle, J. R.
Speech Acts: an essay in the Philosophy of Language. New York: Cambridge University Press, 1969

A crucial distinction made in this work is between the 'sentence' and the 'act' it is used to perform. The unit of linguistic communication is not the symbol, word, or sentence, but the production of those in the performance of an act. Searle sees a theory of language as part of a theory of action, requiring for completeness the study of the role of formal features in speech acts, to complement the independent study of form. The performance of speech acts, it is hypothesized, is made possible by certain rules for the use of linguistic elements. In equating rules for performing speech acts with rules for uttering linguistic elements, i.e. with the rules of meaning of sentences, Searle denies the usual divorce between or exclusive concentration on either sentence meaning or the situated use of expressions. It is insisted, against behaviourist theories of language use, that a speech act is performed in virtue of the conventional meaning of the sentence used. Philosophy, however, is not concerned with the conventional devices for promising, requesting and so on, in a particular language. Searle suggests that those devices include performative verbs, for example 'I promise', intonation, stress, and word order, but he is concerned with underlying rules which provide, for example, for the utterance of any promising device to count as the undertaking of an obligation. The resulting analysis of speech acts is thus in terms of the circumstances, intentions, and expectations which must hold, universally, for a sentence including conventional promising devices to act as a promise. Searle expects that specifications of those presuppositions for the innumerable varieties of speech acts we can refer to with performative verbs such as 'threaten', 'greet', 'request', etc. will be able to be organized into sets of core specifications which will provide a basis for grouping speech acts.

Short, M. H.
'A Stylistic Analysis of Steinbeck's *Of Mice and Men*'. MA thesis, University of Birmingham, 1970

The main area of attention by linguists to how sentences are used and put together into coherent texts has been in the stylistic analysis of literary texts. Stylistics has aimed either to put established techniques of grammatical description at the service of literary criticism or to use the structural methods of linguistics for the analysis of narrative. This thesis bases literary interpretation on syntactic analysis, focusing on the stylistic significance of the selection and distribution of grammatical structures. In relation to the analysis of interactional discourse, of course, the focus of literary text analysis is generally on the internal structuring of what, in interaction, would be a surface discourse function. The interest of this thesis is in its attention not only to narrative but to the conversations between the central characters. Their relationships are discussed in interactive terms, on the basis of their conversational roles and strategies.

Sinclair, J. McH.
'Indescribable English'. Inaugural lecture, University of Birmingham, 1966

A case is argued for the paramount importance of dynamic situational description, an approach to language which emphasizes that we *use language* rather than *say things*, that utterances *do* things rather than just *mean* things. Argument is made for the use of naturalistic tape-recorded data, rather than intuition or informants' reports. Two crucial concepts proposed are, firstly, that of 'situational appropriacy' which is set against 'correctness', and 'situational adequacy' set against 'explicitness', for the task of formulating the object of linguistic study. As an indication of the tasks of discourse analysis, the sequential possibilities following one particular question are discussed. A variety of options are proposed, and related to more general features of discourse such as the holding of initiative in order to control the conversation. It is suggested that some utterances following the question 'How are you enjoying Birmingham?' dislocate the discourse, while other utterances *fit* the predictions of the question. 'Very much thanks' is an example of a good fit; 'Pardon' an example of 'medium trouble'; 'Excuse me a moment please' an example of 'context trouble'; and 'Yes' or 'It's raining' examples of 'dislocation'. Cross-cutting this dimension, a next utterance can be a 'response' or an 'initiative'—question, command, statement, or exclamation. A third factor noted is the possibility of changing the *plane* of the discourse, by referring to the utterance itself. Such replies as 'What do you mean, enjoy?' or 'Are you joking?' *break-up* the discourse by shifting attention from the meaning of the question to the legality of asking it, the intelligibility of it, the purpose for which it was asked and so on. Selections on these three dimensions combine to produce a variety of sequential possibilities after a question.

Skinner, B. F.
Verbal Behaviour. New York: Appleton-Century-Crofts, 1957

This is an approach to the use of language which, in its starting point, explicitly ignores the formal patterning of language and denies that meaning is explicated as rule-governed. It is useful to consider because it approaches the use of language in terms of the function of utterances by a speaker produced in response to a specific environment. Skinner is not concerned at all with language as a structure abstracted out of occasions of use. For

Skinner, verbal behaviour has functions which are discovered solely on the criterion of the circumstances (stimulus) under which that behaviour occurs, and its effects (reinforcement). The unit of verbal behaviour is an operative unit and cannot be linguistically defined. It is for our purpose unfortunate that the main engagement of linguists with Skinner has been in terms of an argument about language learning, in which exclusive positions on the role of underlying rules and environmental conditions have been taken up. Skinner offers an alternative to the cataloguing, on intuitive criteria, of language functions such as the 'expressive'/'referential' functions and to the more systematic but still abstract classifications of philosophy. His classification of functions is based on situated uses of language by single speakers in the presence of an audience. Two of the major functions identified are (1) the 'mand'-behaviour functioning to satisfy the speaker's need for information, an object etc., and (2) the 'tact'-behaviour evoked by a relevant presence in the environment, extending the listener's contact with the environment. Where language is being used in brief, isolated utterances for the purpose of controlling the environment to satisfy one's basic needs, Skinner's classification is usable. Recently it has been used in an analysis of the natural language of two 3-year-old children in their home environment (Horner and Gussow, 1972). Only mands and tacts figured largely in the speech of these children. No 'intraverbal' behaviour was discovered, so no test was made of the possibility of using Skinner's third functional category. The intraverbal function covers cases where the response is to a preceding *verbal* stimulus. For example, Skinner suggests that to such verbal stimuli as 'why?' the learned response is 'because . . .' whatever else may follow. It seems unlikely that extended sequences of language could be adequately analysed within the offered framework which admits only this simple causal relation of one unit of behaviour to another.

Smith, B. O. *et al.*
A Tentative Report on the Strategies of Teaching. Urbana: Bureau of Educational Research, University of Illinois, 1964

The focus of this research is the identification of the types of logical operations performed by teachers and pupils. Three major units of analysis are used: strategy, venture and move. 'Venture' is a set of utterances dealing with a simple topic, and nine different types are recognized, e.g. causal, evaluative, conceptual. 'Moves' are the verbal manoeuvres which make up the different ventures. 'Strategy' includes treatment of subject matter and control of pupil behaviour and strategies can vary according to the types and sequences of moves used. Smith and his colleagues concluded that, in spite of difficulties, they had established analytical categories capable of describing the logical operations of teachers and pupils, and suggest that particularly the notion of strategy can be used in further research relating teacher performance to educational objectives.

Soskin, W. F., and John, V. P.
'A Study of Spontaneous Talk'. In R. Barker (ed.) *Stream of Behavior*. New York: Appleton-Century-Crofts, 1963

Soskin and John, in a study aiming to describe the individual's psychological states in relation to his environment as managed through language, point out the inadequacies of analysing conversational interaction in terms of quantification of occurrences of functional units. The classification of functions used here is a development of the scheme put forward in an earlier behavioural approach to language by Morris (1955). This is supplemented by 'dynamic' analysis which includes a scale of 'locus-direction' of the message, according to which changes in emotional states of the speakers are coded. At the end of their analyses of a wealth of recorded data from natural conversation, Soskin and John doubt whether in fact they have captured the sequential dynamics of episodes in those conversations. The scores produced in their coding cannot reveal the effect on one participant of, for example, a series of mildly provoking remarks, none of which in themselves score highly as derogatory or accusatory. Their effect depends on being part of a larger sequence, which Soskin and John had no tools to analyse.

Speier, M.
'Some Conversational Problems for Interactional Analysis'. In D. Sudnow (ed.), 1972

Speier is concerned with how talk is generated in a particular situation, that of a family meal. Talk is an adjunct to the activity of eating a meal, which could be accomplished in silence. The talk that does occur is of two kinds: firstly, talk related to the practical activity of conducting the progress of a meal, which is in part organized by the natural progression of the meal. 'Family meals are projects managed by adult participants, (who) formulate their conversation around the practical tasks of running the meal for the children. Likewise, the children formulate their speech for the adults whom they recognize as controlling the activity.' Secondly, there occurs talk on a 'topic', which is not necessarily bound to the practical activity, though that may provide resources for 'topical' conversation.

Turner, R.
'Some formal properties of therapy talk'. In D. Sudnow (ed.), 1972

Turner discusses a situation which is constituted by a particular kind of talk. Although group therapy usually occurs in a particular place and certain participants, in particular the therapist, must be present, the talk that occurs there is not all therapy talk (just as classroom talk is not all 'teaching'). Turner discusses how a break is made between 'preliminary conversation' and the scheduled activity of 'therapy', and the ways in which routine conversational properties are transformed in therapy talk. A major feature of therapy talk is the refusal of the therapist to give any evaluation of how the 'patients' are doing. He refuses to tell them what they should be getting out of the therapy. In terms of actual sequences of talk the therapist is seen to avoid 'second actions', e.g. to refuse to answer questions.

Turner, R. H.
'Role Taking: Process versus Conformity'. In A. M. Rose (ed.) *Human Behaviour and Social Process*. London: Routledge & Kegan Paul, 1962

Within sociology the impetus to study interaction rather than, or as well as, the structuring of society in terms of larger social groupings arises mainly from the symbolic interactionist perspective. A major concern within that perspective has been to define the concept of 'role', a concept mediating between the social structure and the individual actor. According to theorists such as Turner, role is to be seen not as a stable set of expectations, rights and duties, determined by social structure and determining the behaviour of an actor playing that role, but as a situational identity negotiated through interaction with others. The focus on interaction is thus linked to a theoretical debate on how social order is sustained. Interaction is studied as a process of creating and defining one's role in the presence of others, and in turn having one's role defined by those others. In fact, in empirical studies, instances of this process are usually simply indicated, rather than the process being studied in detail through a sustained encounter.

Waimon, M. D., and Hermanowicz, H. J.
'A conceptual system for prospective teachers to study teaching behaviour'. Paper presented to the American Educational Research Association in Chicago. Normal: Illinois State University, 1965

This research aims to provide a system to analysis usable by prospective teachers for the analysis of classroom behaviour. The analytic categories focus on the teachers' behaviour, and are dominated by a concept of learning in which the teacher attempts to promote learning by (a) developing a predisposition for learning, (b) helping pupils to acquire, comprehend or use subject matter, and (c) giving evaluative reactions to pupil responses. The pupil responses are analysed according to 'adequacy', in terms of the teacher's expectations, and 'magnitude', in terms of the level of knowledge, comprehension, or reasoning exhibited. Additionally, it is proposed that the classroom discourse can be analysed in terms of larger units or 'teaching episodes'.

Watzlawick, P., Beavin, J. H., and Jackson, D. D.
Pragmatics of Human Communication. New York: Norton, 1967

The authors attempt, on the basis of their experience of the distorted communication sequences in the families of schizophrenic patients, to develop a model of the pragmatics of human communication to which pathological communication can be related. A text from a play about family life is analysed in order to illustrate how family members are part of an interactional system in which their relationships are defined. The rules and tactics of the interactional game played by the participants are described in terms of formal features of sequencing—initiation, punctuation, and closure of episodes—in their interaction. Though the content of family arguments vary it is pointed out that the structure repeats itself, and each exchange is seen to limit the next move in the game. Here then some of the formal structures of interaction are being attended to, using concepts of a *game*, made up of *exchanges* and *moves*. The exchanges in this game are constituted largely by a series of commands and insults since neither participant will take the subordinate role of accepting an initiative from the other. Tacitly relied on is a notion of normal communication in which, for example, it is known that commands are initiatives which require a response not a re-initiative.

Wight, J., and Norris, R. A.
Teaching English to West Indian Children. Schools Council Working Paper no. 29, London: Evans Methuen, 1970.

This is a report on the research stage of a project designed to develop language teaching materials for West Indian children in British schools. A number of tests were used to determine the major factors affecting the English learning abilities of West Indian schoolchildren. The research focused not merely on the extent to which grammatical, lexical and phonological differences between Creole and standard English impeded the children's language learning, but on how the children differed from native pupils on their general oral fluency and skill at communication. It was for problems in this second area that the bulk of the teaching materials were finally developed. Although the researchers were not able to make a systematic investigation, they postulate that such factors as the attitudes to language, evaluations of linguistic skills, balance of verbal and non-verbal communication, and family communication patterns and the child's role within this, in the West Indian community are crucial influences on the West Indian child's communicative performance.

REFERENCES

Unless otherwise indicated, all of the dates refer to the editions consulted.

Abercrombie, D. *Problems and Principles in Language Study*. London: Longman, 1963.
— *Elements of General Phonetics*. Edinburgh: Edinburgh University Press, 1967.
Albrow, K. H. *The Rhythm and Intonation of Spoken English*. Schools Council Programme in Linguistics and English Teaching, Paper 9. London: Longman, 1968.
Ardener, E. (ed.) *Social Anthropology and Linguistics*. Association of Social Anthropologists, Monograph 10, 1969.
Austin, J. L. *How to do things with words*. Oxford: Clarendon Press, 1962.
Bales, R. F. *Interaction Process Analysis*. Reading, Mass: Addison Wesley, 1951.
Barnes, D. 'Language in the Secondary Classroom'. In D. Barnes, J. Britton and H. Rosen, *Language, the Learner and the School*. Harmondsworth: Penguin Books, 1969.
Barthes, F. 'Introduction à l'analyse structural des récits'. *Communications* 8, 1966.
Bateson, G. 'Toward a Theory of Schizophrenia'. *Behavioural Science* 1.
Bellack, A. A., Kliebard, H. M., Hyman, R. T., and Smith, F. L. *The Language of the Classroom*. New York: Teachers College Press, 1966.
Bernstein, B. 'Linguistic Codes, Hesitation Phenomena and Intelligence'. *Language and Speech* 5.1.1962. pp. 31–48.
— 'Social Class, Linguistic Codes and Grammatical Elements'. *Language and Speech* 5.4.1962. pp. 231–40.
— 'Elaborated and Restricted Codes: their Social Origins and some Consequences'. *American Anthropologist* 66. 6.2. 1964. pp. 55–69.
— 'A Socio-linguistic Approach to Socialisation'. In J. J. Gumperz and D. Hymes (eds.), 1972.
Bloomfield, L. *Language*. New York: Holt, Rinehart, Winston, 1933.
Boesen, M. T. 'Developing Maturity in Writing'. *The Instructor* 23. 1966. pp. 103–7.
Boyd, J., and Thorne, J. P. 'The Semantics of Modal Verbs'. In *Journal of Linguistics* Vol. 5. 1969. pp. 57–74.
Brazil, D. C. *Intonation in Discourse* (in preparation).
Bright, W. (ed.) *Sociolinguistics*. The Hague: Mouton, 1966.
Candlin, C. N. 'Acquiring Communicative Competence'. Paper given at the 32nd. Dutch Philologists' Conference, Utrecht, April 1972. (unpublished).

Cazden, C. V. J., John V. P., and Hymes, D. (eds.) *Functions of Language in the Classroom*. New York: Teachers College Press, 1972.

Chatman, S. 'Analysing Narrative Structure'. *Language and Style* 2. 1969. pp. 3–36.

Chomsky, N. *Aspects of the Theory of Syntax*. Cambridge, Mass.: MIT Press, 1965.

Cicourel, A. 'Ethnomethodology'. In T. A. Sebeok *et al.* (ed.) *Current Trends in Linguistics* 12 (forthcoming).

Coulthard, R. M. 'An Empirical Investigation of Restricted and Elaborated Codes'. PhD. thesis, University of Birmingham, 1970.

Ervin-Tripp, S. 'Sociolinguistics'. In L. Berkowitz (ed.) *Advances in Experimental Social Psychology*. New York: Academic Press Inc., 1969. 4. pp. 91–165.

Firbas, J. 'Thoughts on the Communicative Function of the Verb in English, German and Czech'. *Brno Studies in English* 1. 1959. pp. 39–63.

— 'On Defining the Theme in Functional Sentence Analysis'. *Travaux Linguistiques de Prague* 1. 1964. pp. 267–80.

Firth, J. R. 'The techniques of Semantics'. 1935. In *Papers in Linguistics 1934–1951*. London: Oxford University Press, 1957. pp. 7–33.

Fishman, J. A. 'Who speaks what language, to whom and when'. *La Linguistique* 2. 1965. pp. 67–88.

Flanders, N. A. *Teacher Influence, Pupil Attitudes and Achievement*. Co-operative Research Monographs. No. 12. U.S. Office of Education. U.S. Govt. Printing Offices, 1965.

— *Analysing Teaching Behaviour*. Reading, Mass.: Addison-Wesley, 1970.

Fries, C. C. *The Structure of English*. London: Longman, 1957.

Frake, C. O. 'Struck by Speech: the Yakan concept of Litigation'. In L. Nader (ed.) *Law in Culture and Society*. Chicago: Aldine Publishing Co., 1969.

Gallagher, J. J., and Aschner, M. J. 'A Preliminary Report on Analyses of Classroom Interaction'. *Merrill-Palmer Quarterly* Vol. 9. 1963. pp. 183–94.

Garfinkel, H. *Studies in Ethnomethodology*. Englewood Cliffs, N.J.: Prentice-Hall, 1967.

—, and Sacks, H. 'On Formal Structures of Practical Actions'. In J. C. McKinney and E. Tiryakian (eds.) *Theoretical Sociology*. New York: Appleton-Century-Crofts, 1969.

Geertz, C. *The Religion of Java*. Glencoe: The Free Press, 1960.

Goffman, E. *Encounters*. Indianapolis: Bobbs-Merrill, 1961.

— *Behavior in Public Places*. New York: Free Press, 1963.

— 'The Neglected Situation'. In J. Gumperz and D. Hymes (eds.), 1964.

— *Interaction Ritual*. Chicago: Aldine Publishing Co., 1967.

Gordon, D., and Lakoff, G. 'Conversational Postulates'. In *Papers from the 7th Regional Meeting*. Chicago: Chicago Linguistic Society, 1971.

Gumperz, J. J. 'Hindi-Punjabi code-switching in Delhi'. In H. G. Lunt (ed.) *Proceedings of the 9th. International Congress of Linguistics*. The Hague: Mouton, 1964.

— 'Linguistic and Social Interaction in two Communities'. In J. Gumperz and D. Hymes (eds.), 1964.

—, and Herasimchuk, E. 'The Conversational Analysis of Social Meaning: a study of classroom interaction'. Mimeographed. Berkeley: University of California, 1972.

—, and Hymes, D. (eds.) *Directions in Sociolinguistics*. New York: Holt, Rinehart, Winston, 1972.

Habermas, J. 'Toward a Theory of Communicative Competence'. In P. Dreitzel (ed.) *Recent Sociology* 2. London: Collier-Macmillan, 1971.

Halliday, M. A. K. 'Categories of the Theory of Grammar'. *Word* 17. 1961. pp. 241–92.

— 'The concept of rank: a reply'. *Journal of Linguistics* 2. 1966.

— 'Notes on Transitivity and Theme in English'. *Journal of Linguistics* 3, 1967. pp. 37–81, 199–245. 4. 1968. pp. 179–215.

— 'Language Structure and Language Function'. In J. Lyons (ed.) *New Horizons in Linguistics*. Harmondsworth: Penguin Books, 1970.

— 'Language in a Social Perspective'. *Educational Review* 23. 3. 1971. pp. 165–88.

Halliday, M. A. K., McIntosh, A., and Strevens, P. *The Linguistic Sciences and Language Teaching*. London: Longman, 1964.

Harris, Z. 'Discourse Analysis'. *Language* 28. 1952. pp. 1–30.

— 'Discourse Analysis: a sample text'. *Language* 28. 1952. pp. 474–94.

Hasan, R. *Grammatical Cohesion in Spoken and Written English*. Part I. Schools Council Programme in Linguistics and English Teaching. Paper 7. London: Longman, 1968. Part II (forthcoming).

Horner, V. M., and Gussow, J. D. 'John and Mary: a pilot study in linguistic ecology'. In C. Cazden, V. P. John and D. Hymes, *Functions of Language in the Classroom*. New York: Teachers College Press, 1972.

Huddlestone, R. D., Hudson, R. A., Winter, E. O., and Hernnie, A. *Sentence and Clause in Scientific English*. O.S.T.I. Report No. 5030, 1968.

Hymes, D. 'The Ethnography of Speaking'. In T. Gladwin and W. C. Sturtevant (eds.) *Anthropology and Human Behaviour*. Washington: Anthropological Society of Washington, 1962. pp. 13–53.

— 'Directions in Etho-linguistic Theory'. In A. K. Romney and R. G. D'Andrade (eds.) *Transcultural Studies in Cognition. American Anthropologist* 66. 3. Part 2. 1964. pp. 6–56.

— 'Introduction: Toward Ethnographies of Communication'. In J. J. Gumperz and D. Hymes (eds.), 1964. pp. 1–34.

— 'Models of the Interaction of Language and Social Setting'. *Journal of Social Issues* 23. 2. 1967. pp. 8–28.

— 'On Communicative Competence'. Mimeographed. University of

Pennsylvania, 1972.

— 'Introduction'. In C. B. Cazden, V. P. John, and D. Hymes (eds.), 1972.

Jakobson, R. 'Closing Statement: Linguistics and Poetics'. In T. A. Sebeok (ed.), 1960, pp. 350–77.

Jefferson, G. 'Side Sequences'. In D. Sudnow (ed.), 1972.

Joos, M. *The Five Clocks*. New York: Harbinger Books, 1967.

Katz, J., and Fodor, J. 'The structure of a Semantic Theory'. *Language* 39. 1963. pp. 170–210.

—, and Postal, P. M. *An Integrated Theory of Linguistic Descriptions*. Cambridge, Mass.: M.I.T. Press, 1964.

Labov, W. 'Phonological Correlates of Social Stratification'. *American Anthropologist* 66. 1964. pp. 164–76.

— *The Social Stratification of English in New York City*. Washington: Center for Applied Linguistics, 1966.

— 'The Effect of Social Mobility on Linguistic Behaviour'. In S. Lieberson (ed.), 1967.

— 'The Study of Language in its Social Context'. *Studium Generale* 23. 1970. pp. 30–87.

— 'Rules for Ritual Insults'. In D. Sudnow (ed.), 1972.

Labov, W., and Weletzky, J. 'Narrative Analysis: Oral Versions of Personal Experience'. In J. Helm (ed.) *Essays on the Verbal and Visual Arts*. American Ethnological Society. Annual Spring Meeting. Philadelphia, 1966. Seattle, 1967.

Lakoff, R. 'Language in Context'. In *Language* 48. 1972.

Lamb, S. M. *Outline of Stratification Grammar*. Washington D.C.: Georgetown University Press, 1966.

Lawton, D. *Social Class, Language and Education*. London: Routledge & Kegan Paul, 1968.

Lieberson, S. 'Explorations in Sociolinguistics'. *International Journal of Applied Linguistics* 33. 4. 1967.

Malinowski, B. *Coral Gardens and their Magic, a Study of the Methods of Tilling the Soil and of Agricultural Rites in the Trobriand Islands*. Vol. 2. *The Language of Magic and Gardening*. London: Allen & Unwin, 1935.

McCawley, J. D. 'Where do noun phrases come from?' In R. A. Jacobs and P. S. Rosenbaum (eds.) *Readings in English Transformational Grammar*. Waltham, Mass.: Ginn & Co., 1970.

Matthews, P. H. 'The concept of rank in "neo-Firthian" grammar'. *Linguistics* 2. 1966.

Mitchell, T. F. 'The Language of Buying and Selling in Cyrenaica'. *Hesperis* 44. 1 and 2. 1957. pp. 31–71.

Morton, Rev. A. Q. 'The authorship of Greek prose'. *Journal of the Royal Statistical Society* 1965.

Pearce, R. D. 'The Structure of Discourse in Broadcast Interviews'. M.A. thesis, University of Birmingham, 1973.

Pride, J. B. 'Analysing Classroom Procedures'. In H. Fraser and W. R.

O'Donnell (eds.) *Applied Linguistics and the Teaching of English*. London: Longman, 1969.

— *The Social Meaning of Language*. London: Oxford University Press, 1971.

Quirk, R., and Greenbaum, S. *Elicitation Experiments in English*. London: Longman, 1971.

Ross, J. R. 'On declarative sentences'. In R. A. Jacobs and P. S. Rosenbaum *Readings in English Transformational Grammar*. Waltham, Mass.: Ginn & Co., 1970.

Rubin, J. 'Bilingual Usage in Paraguay'. In J. A. Fishman (ed.) *Readings in the Sociology of Language*. The Hague: Mouton, 1968.

Sacks, H. 'An Initial Investigation of the Usability of Conversational Data for Doing Sociology'. In D. Sudnow (ed.), 1972.

— 'On the analysability of stories by children'. In J. J. Gumperz and D. Hymes (eds.), 1972.

Schegloff, E. A. 'Sequencing in Conversational Openings'. *American Anthropologist* 70. 6. 1968. pp. 1075–95.

— 'Notes on a Conversational Practice: Formulating Place'. In D. Sudnow (ed.), 1972. pp. 75–119.

—, and Sacks, H. 'Opening up Closings' *Semiotica* VIII, 1973.

Searle, J. R. *Speech Acts: An Essay in the Philosophy of Language*. New York: Cambridge University Press, 1969.

Short, M. H. 'A Stylistic Analysis of John Steinbeck's *Of Mice and Men*'. M.A. thesis, University of Birmingham, 1970.

Sinclair, J. McH. 'Indescribable English'. Inaugural lecture, University of Birmingham, 1966. (unpublished).

— 'Taking a poem to pieces'. In R. Fowler (ed.) *Essays on Style and Language*. London: Routledge & Kegan Paul, 1966.

— 'A technique of stylistic description'. In *Language and Style* I. No. 4. 1968.

— 'Parlotactics'. Paper delivered to the Leeds Linguistic Society, November 1968.

— *A Course in Spoken English: Grammar*. London: Oxford University Press, 1972. 'Linguistics in Colleges of Education'. *Dudley Educational Journal* I, 3. 1973.

Skinner, B. F. *Verbal Behavior*. New York: Appleton, 1957.

Smith, B. O. *et al. A Tentative Report on the Strategies of Teaching*. U.S. Department of Health, Education and Welfare. Office of Education. Co-operative Research Project No. 1640. Urbana: Bureau of Educational Research, University of Illinois, 1964.

Soskin, W. F., and John, V. P. 'A Study of Spontaneous Talk'. In R. Barker (ed.) *Stream of Behaviour*. New York: Appleton-Century-Crofts, 1963.

Speier, M. 'Some Conversational Problems for Interactional Analysis'. In D. Sudnow (ed.), 1972.

Sudnow, D. (ed.) *Studies in Social Interaction*. New York: Free Press, 1972.

Taba, H., Levine, S., and Elzey, F. F. *Thinking in Elementary School Children.* U.S. Dept. of Health, Education and Welfare. Office of Education. Co-operative Research Project No. 1574. San Francisco State College, 1964.

Thorne, J. P. Invited lectures, Department of Extramural Studies, University of Birmingham, 1973

Todorov, K. 'Les catégories du récit litteraire', *Communications* 8. 1966.

Turner, R. 'Some Formal Properties of Therapy Talk'. In D. Sudnow (ed.), 1972. pp. 367–96.

Turner, R. H. 'Role Taking: Process versus Conformity'. In A. M. Rose (ed.), pp. 20–40.

Vachek, J. *The Linguistic School of Prague.* Bloomington: Indiana University Press, 1966.

Waimon, M. D., and Hermanowicz, H. J. 'A Conceptual System for Prospective Teachers to Study Teaching Behavior'. Paper presented to the American Educational Research Association in Chicago. Normal: Illinois State University, 1965.

Watzlawick, P., Beavin, J. H., and Jackson, D. D. *Pragmatics of Human Communication.* New York: Norton, 1967.

Wells, G. *Interim Report of Pilot Study.* S.S.R.C. Project on 'Language Development in the Pre-School Child'. Mimeographed. University of Bristol School of Education, 1972.

Widdowson, H. G. 'The Teaching of Rhetoric to Students of Science and Technology'. C.I.L.T. Reports and Papers. 7. London, 1971. pp. 31–40.

Wight, J., and Norris, R. A. *Teaching English to West Indian Children.* Schools Council Working Paper No. 29. London: Evans Methuen, 1970.

Weinreich, U. 'Explorations in Semantic Theory'. In T. A. Sebeok (ed.) *Current Trends in Linguistics.* Vol. 3. The Hague: Mouton, 1966.

Wittgenstein, L. *Philosophical Investigations.* London: Oxford University Press, 1953.

Texts A, B, C, D, and E
These constitute the initial sample used by the Project, controlled for subject matter, age and ability of the children, and size of the group. They were taught by their class teachers, using materials based on Egyptian hieroglyphs.

Text F
The first part of a double lesson with a mixed class of thirty-one pupils aged between thirteen and fourteen, at a West Midland Comprehensive School. They were taken by a visiting teacher in a discussion of attitudes to language.

Text G
A class of ten-year-olds in a junior school taken by one of the teachers at the school in a science lesson, on the subject of energy.

Text H
An extract from a lesson in which a class of eight-year-olds are taught by a teacher who is new to them, using materials prepared by the Schools Council Project for the Teaching of English to West Indian children.

Text I
Desultory conversation recorded in Edinburgh University for the purposes of research into lexical collocation.

KING ALFRED'S COLLEGE

LIBRARY